Anatomy of a Moonshine Town

Anatomy

of a

Moonshine
Town

Still Remembered

Betty J. Hartshorn

XULON PRESS

Xulon Press
2301 Lucien Way #415
Maitland, FL 32751
407.339.4217
www.xulonpress.com

Paperback ISBN-13: 978-1-6628-5316-6
Hard Cover ISBN-13: 978-1-6628-5317-3

FOREWORD

efore Prohibition, most people knew very little about Beavertown. In fact, it was not even on maps of the time. Not that it bothered Beavers. Up to then, they lived much as they had been taught by their town's founder and maker, "Dragon John" Beaver. But that was about to change. This book was written to show just how that change came about.

Before the war (World War I) Beavertown was an agrarian society, living off the land and running various enterprises like the mussel industry. Building the dam gave them a taste of what it was like making real money. Sadly, that was the last real hard cash they would see.

While the rest of the country was "living it up" in the twenties, Beavertown was slowly going under. But for the sale of "moonshine," there might be no Beavertown today. This book covers the rise and near down fall of the little town.

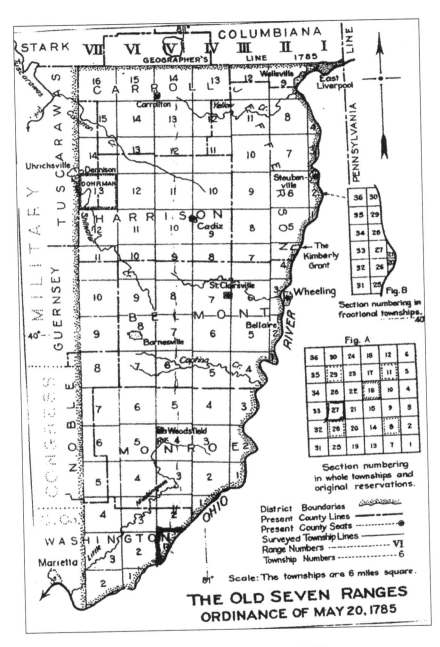

THE OLD SEVEN RANGES

Very Early Photo of Beavertown

CHAPTER 1

*O*n July 3, 1992, *The Marietta Times* published an article titled, "Communities full of history," with some surprising facts about Washington County's towns and villages.

As the first organized settlement in the Northwest Territory, Marietta occupies a unique place in the history of the county, and volumes have been written about the "Pioneer City." Cutler also enjoys a degree of fame—locally, for sure—for its service as a station on the Underground Railroad prior to the Civil War. Thousands of slaves passed through there on their way to freedom just across the river in the North.

Most surprising, Macksburg. Back in 1884, the very first oil well in Ohio was drilled there. People flocked to the little town, increasing its population to almost three thousand.

Most tragic, Watertown, whose founder, Abel Waterman, was killed by hostile Indians just six years after settling there.

In the northern most corner of the county sits a little town with a history quite unlike all the others. Had its name been completely left out of the following two paragraphs, most readers of the *Times* could have recognized it instantly.

A mix of riverside bungalows and trailers, underground house, two taverns, a service station and a little white church along the Ohio River make up Beavertown, once a notorious moonshine town.

Folks in this mile long hamlet along Ohio 7, three miles south of Matamoras, still are full of stories about illicit whiskey made during prohibition in the wooded hills overlooking the Ohio. Today, about 75–100 residents call Beavertown home.

And notorious it was. For thirteen years, the tiny hamlet may have produced as much—or more—illegal whiskey per capita than many bigger, more sophisticated operations in the country.

By Prohibition's end, Beavertown and whiskey had become practically synonymous—and remained so, though stills and mash barrels have been gone from the surrounding hills and hollows for almost a century.

Beavertown certainly was not the only place making alcoholic beverages in those days. Just a few miles down-river in Cincinnati, former Chicago pharmacist, George Remus, ran one of the biggest and most productive illegal whiskey operations in the country.

In league with city officials and law enforcement, he ran his business like a proper captain of industry. Supporting the arts and giving generously to worthy causes, he hosted lavish parties attended by the cream of Cincinnati society.

Until Edward Behr published his book, *Prohibition*, in 1996, most folks were totally unaware of that period in the "Queen City's" past. Caused quite a stir for a bit, but in the end, all the hoopla soon died down. "Her Majesty" just shook the dirt off her skirts, straightened her crown and continued on her merry way.

Yet little Beavertown—which would barely fill one of Cincinnati's back streets—has never been able to leave its past behind.

Granted, headlines like "WHISKEY PACKIN' MAMA" (lady arrested for selling drinks out of her kitchen) are pretty hard to forget. Over the years there were many, many more.

When Prohibition ended on December 5, 1933, Beavertown dutifully abandoned its stills, expecting to return to its former state of relative anonymity. Never happened. Beavertown had left a lasting impression on America's readers.

A lady who lives up in Lancaster, Ohio, still remembers reading about "the little town that made all that whiskey" in her local newspaper. Might well have been the article which Roger Kalter wrote back in September of 1988. (Although there have been many others.)

Kalter's article, "Beavertown: a spirited history," gave readers a good idea of what life was like there in Prohibition times. Of course, by then all of the original "moonshiners" were gone, but the following generation still had memories of that time.

Outsiders were not much help. Even county historian, Jerry Devol, knew little of what actually happened in Beavertown during those days. Except for one incident involving a cousin, Constable "Fax" Devol.

Receiving a call to investigate a complaint about some "moonshine" operation up around Beavertown, the constable dutifully traveled the thirty miles up Route Seven to "nose around." They took his gun, his clothes, threw him out of a row boat and told him never to come back.

Devol also knew of a pilot, L.H. "Scotty" Scot, who made a lot of money selling Beavertown whiskey. Landing in a field or small landing strip, he would load up with "moonshine" and take off. Local police had no jurisdiction over airplanes.

Another pilot, known only as "Covey," often landed in a hayfield just across the highway from the John Hutchison house. Leaving his plane unguarded, he would take off for Beavertown. Sometimes staying for extended periods of time. Neighborhood kids had a great time "flying" in the open cockpit of "Cubby's" plane.

Covey once invited one of his Beaver lady friends up "for a spin." She took him up on his offer, climbed aboard and off they went. During the flight, she happened to notice that some parts of the plane were actually held together with wire. No more plane rides for her.

While Devol was right about the airplane whiskey operation, he was sadly misinformed when it came to the rest of Beavertown's history. No way was Beavertown "named for Michael Beaver back in the 1790's." (Although there would have been no Beavertown without Michael.)

In the 1790's Michael Beaver was only about six years old, living with his family over in old feudal Germany. Besides that, there was no Beavertown then at all. Not until Michael's son John moved over to a strip of land along the Ohio River.

Eileen Thomas (Michael Beaver's great, great, great granddaughter) wrote in her column for *Washington Co. Ohio to 1980*, "Simple truth is, Beavertown derived its name from the fact that everyone in the village has the family name of Beaver, or is related."

After 1992, *The Times* appeared to be done with Beavertown. But in March of 2003, under its continuing feature, "Time Past," little snippets like these began to appear:

March 24, 2003—75 years ago.
A series of liquor raids made at Beavertown by county and state enforcement officers resulted in the confiscation of more than 35 active stills, hundreds of barrels of mash and large quantities of whiskey and beer, and the arrest of two men, Bryan Beaver and Bud Manson, who are held at the county jail.

February 2, 2006—75 years ago.
The sheriff's men destroyed three whiskey camps in the hills near Beavertown as part of a mopping up campaign in eastern Washington County. They dynamited three stills and captured 16 gallons of whiskey.

March 1, 2006—75 years ago.
Men from the sheriff's department continued their raids on whiskey camps in the Beavertown section, destroying three stills, 1,100 gallons of mash and 40 gallons of finished whiskey.

March 20, 2007—75 years ago.
Federal prohibition officers and men from the sheriff's department made a raid at Beavertown which resulted in the seizure of 143 gallons of whiskey and 650 gallons of mash.

Little doubt that *The Times* played a big part in putting Beavertown on the map. Especially in and around the Ohio Valley. But its area of circulation hardly reached into cities like Chicago.

Matamoras resident, Franklin Holdren, drove buses for Greyhound Bus Lines during that time. Had just finished a run into the "Windy City." Chatting with the little group gathered there, mentioned that he lived down in the Ohio Valley. Immediately struck a chord of recognition for one old fellow. "Anywhere near that little 'moonshine' town on the river?"

Sound far-fetched? Wait. In the 1950's, a family of Beavers, for various reasons, moved all the way out to California. At last, an end of all that whiskey business.

Then, as they were being introduced at a neighborhood gathering, one elderly gentleman, shaking hands, said "Beaver, Beaver. You couldn't be from that little place that made all that whiskey, could you?"

Distance, age, gender. Makes no difference. At a public auction in the 1980's, auctioneer Alvis Weddle, putting some empty gallon jugs up for bids, spotted a little gray-haired Beaver lady sitting in the crowd. "Grandma," he laughed, "I bet you coulda used summa these."

She "coulda" for sure. She and her husband had run one of Beavertown's most productive "moonshine" operations, serving customers from as far away as the state capitol. Never hurt her, for she lived to see her one hundredth birthday—even a bit beyond. Now lies buried up in Parr Hill Cemetery along with all the other "moonshiners" whose "spirits" continue to "haunt" those left behind.

Passing of the eighteenth (Prohibition) amendment meant little to Beavers. They were having trouble just "keeping their heads above water." Not that they were starving. Like most farmers, they had plenty to eat. But no hard cash with which to put "shoes on their kids' feet and clothes on their backs."

Yet the rest of the country was booming. This description of that period from *World Book Encyclopedia*:

The United States set off on a joy ride in an "era of wonderful nonsense." Americans felt lighthearted after the war. Henry Ford led the way by "putting America on wheels" in his "Model T." People spent more and more money for good roads, travel and travel resorts.

Up to that point, alcohol had been as much a part of American society as "Mom and apple pie." No amount of legislation was going to change that. So the stage was set, with opportunists like George Remus, waiting in the wings to satisfy the demand which was sure to come.

The chance of making money like that never even occurred to Beavers.

CHAPTER 2

hiskey days are but a small part of Beavertown's history. Yes, Beavertown does have a history. One which follows much the same pattern as all others in Washington County. One which had its beginning way back in old war-torn Germany.

At that time, only Indians and dam building beavers inhabited the Valley. First land to be cleared there was the old Dickerson farm. A man named David Shepherd built a cabin there in "very early times." Later sold it to a Kinsey Dickerson and moved on. The deed conveying the land to Dickerson was recorded in 1796.

That year, 1796, found Beaver forefathers (at various times and places, spelled Bieber, Beeber or Bever) living across the ocean in old feudal Germany. Napoleonic Wars had left Europe in ruins—Germany, in particular.

A series of haphazard governments had succeeded only in making things worse. Raising taxes and mishandling the economy. Feudal landlords were demanding higher and higher rents and even the old Catholic Church, its tithes as well. Something had to give—and did.

A mass exodus began. "At first a trickle, then a flood." In that first trickle, a family of Bevers—father, mother and nine children. Only America held out any hope for survival, so they packed up their meager belongings and headed for the nearest seaport.

How did they know about America? For some time, recruiting agents from the United States had been canvassing Europe in an effort to lure workers to farm its lands and run its factories.

According to Beaver family history (by I.M Beaver, published in 1936), Beavers came from Alsace Loraine, some from Hirschland and other parts of Germany.

Nothing is known about their trip to the coast. Considering conditions in that country, could not have been easy. Voyage across the Atlantic, even worse. Accommodations were crude and overcrowded.

Immigrants were packed into small sailing vessels, capable of holding anywhere from one to four hundred. Many perished along the way, but all eleven Bevers arrived safely. "Locating for a time in Maryland," home to a large concentration of German immigrants. A rich farming area, big attraction for Bevers who had never known anything else.

Bever children grew to adulthood there, married and had children of their own. Might never have left but for the lure of cheap—even free—land in the newly opened Northwest Territory. Along with the thousands heading west, went eight of the Bever children.

At first, land sold by sections (640 acres at $1.25 per acre), but by 1832, became available in forty-acre plots. Many settlers by-passed the hilly Monroe County area in favor of better land farther on, so land there was much cheaper; even free. May be the reason for Bevers choosing to settle there.

According to Marietta Land Office Records, Peter was the first to purchase land there. Followed by the six at various times.

NAME:	Tracts:	Dates of Purchase:
Peter Bever	3	January 15, 1833
		March 30, 1833
		September 4, 1835
John Bever	3	August 27, 1833
	2	April 25, 1836
Michael Bever	1	February 6, 1834
Washington Bever	2	September 26, 1834
		December 22, 1835
Joseph Bever	2	October 2, 1834
		December 3, 1835
Henry Bever	1	June 9, 1836
Nancy Bever	2	September 14, 1836

Aside from price, Bevers may have had another equally important reason for choosing the Monroe County area. Many German immigrants had already settled there. As early as 1819, several German-Swiss families came down the Ohio River and put down roots in Monroe. That area is still largely populated by folks of German descent.

Traveling to the Ohio country from the East was not for the faint-hearted. Only passable routes were mere wagon trails. Horse or oxen drawn wagons, the mode of transportation. Worse, travelers had to wait for rainy season (Spring or Fall) in order to arrive in Pittsburgh when the Ohio River was at flood stage. Then and only then would the river be deep enough to accommodate flatboats—the main means of transportation.

Henry Howe's *Historical Recollections of Ohio* contains the following description of a trip from the East to Pittsburgh:

Whoever went to Ohio from the East had to provide his own carriage and take care of his own baggage. At the time there was really but one highway from the East to the West, that was the great Pennsylvania route from Philadelphia to Pittsburgh. It professed to be a turnpike, but was really only a passable road, and on the mountains narrow and dangerous.

It was chiefly traversed by the wagoners, who carried goods from Philadelphia to the West. A private carriage and driver such as my father had to have, was the abhorrence of the wagoners who considered it simply an evidence of aristocracy.

CHAPTER 3

*T*he Pittsburgh which greeted Bever eyes must have seemed barely civilized after living in eastern cities. Hogs roamed freely throughout the city. Newly arriving wagons lurched along unpaved streets, escorted by yapping dogs. Half-naked Indians, lounging here and there, a common sight.

On market days (Wednesdays and Saturdays), the city took on a carnival-like appearance. Carts and wagons with merchandise lined up all along the main "drag." Smells of animal skins, tallow, bee's wax and maple sugar combined with the over-all haze to give the city a distinctive smoke-housey flavor.

Immigrants lingered in Pittsburgh only as long as it took to sell their wagons and purchase flatboats for their trip down river. Called "sneak boxes" or "the boat that never came back," flatboats were simple rafts built of "anything that would float." One section for shelter. Remaining space held personal belongings, household goods and even livestock.

**Marietta reinactment of a flat boat trip down the Ohio River,
Courtesy of the Marietta Times**

**Replica of a flatboat at the Ohio River Museum in Marietta, Ohio,
built in 1975 and rebuilt in 1996. Based on the design of boats used to
bring the American pioneers to the Northwest Territory in 1788.**

Prices for houseboats started at thirty-five dollars—with a fireplace, forty-five. Guide books were available. Most famous, *The Navigator*, by Zadok Kramer. Not really of much use, for the old Ohio at flood times was never the same for any two seasons.

Little wonder that some never made it to their final destinations. Flood waters were so muddy that shoals, sandbars, sunken trees and other hazards were completely hidden. Whirlpools and eddies made steering a real challenge.

Staying out in the middle of the river was absolutely necessary. Flatboats were favorite targets of Indians and river pirates who used every trick in the book to lure boats to shore. Those who fell for such tricks were robbed and generally murdered. More than one flatboat left Pittsburgh never to be seen again.

On reaching their destinations, flatboats were torn apart and materials used to erect temporary shelters. Often incorporated into permanent dwellings. Those old flatboats paid for themselves many times over.

All seven Bevers survived that perilous trip over the mountain and down the Ohio. Landed somewhere on Monroe County's twenty–nine–mile river fringe. There they prepared for the trek up over those rock hills. Straight up!

In 1846, Henry Howe, carrying a fourteen–pound knapsack, made that same trip up over the hills to Woodsfield, Ohio. Described his trip like this:

A steamboat had landed me on the Ohio some 16 miles away and I came up the hills meeting scarcely a soul or seeing much else than hills and trees. Woodsfield was much out of the world. Indeed the entire county was quite primitive; its people largely dwelt in cabins.

Some of those cabins may well have belonged to Bevers. Except for Henry, who had stuck it out but a year or so, then moved down to Wheeling, Virginia. (West Virginia was still part of the state of Virginia then.)

For that matter, would not have seen Michael either. He had lived there but three years when a Mr. Ice suddenly appeared, accusing him of "jumping his claim."

In the Court of Common Pleas, Journal No. 4, Page 108, a suit in chancery was filed on May 30, 1833 — Michael Beaver VS James Ice, Elizabeth Ice and Thomas Evans. However, the next entry states that the case was moved to Washington County, Ohio. Nothing could be found concerning the outcome.

Such occurrences were quite common then. Unauthorized settlements had been popping up all over the Ohio territory ever since the British pulled out. One poor settler, forced to pay for his land twice, when threatened a third time, simply gave up. Sold his belongings and left the territory for good.

This "squatter" problem became so bad that Congress finally had to take steps to eject unauthorized persons from the territory. That task was given to a General Richard Butler who did his very best, but found it quite impossible. In one of his reports, he wrote:

Called at the settlement of Captain Hogland, who we also warned off, his house had also been torn down and rebuilt. We informed him of the impropriety of his conduct which he acknowledged, and seemed very submissive, and promised to remove and warn his neighbors off also.

Michael chose not to contest Ice's claim. Instead, he and brother Daniel, pulled up stakes and vacated the premises. Purchased land down in Washington County. Following entries in the Marietta Land Office records show that both purchased sections of land on Sheets Run.

| Daniel Bever | 1837 Jan. 26 | Range 5 | Township 03 | Section 30 |
| Michael Bever | 1837 Nov. 07 | Range 5 | Township 01 | Section 34 |

However, did not "remove thither" until 1838. Rumor has it that they stopped in Wheeling for a time before moving on to Sheets Run.

Not many folks lived on Sheets Run when the brothers arrived. They built houses on opposite sides of the little stream. Michael chose a little wooded area just behind the Albert Slack property. Daniel, a plot atop the hill across from Michael.

Neither Daniel nor Michael ever left Sheets Run. Both died and were buried there. Michael, just a few yards from the Slack house, not far off Sheet's Run Road. Two ancient cedars mark the exact spot of Michael and Catherine's resting place. Leaning against the trunk, two headstones, each bearing a barely discernable inscription:

Michael Beaver Died July 28 1860
Catherine Beaver Wife of Michael Beaver Died September 5 1858
Aged 61 Years 9 Months 25 Days

(In accordance with research by Eileen Thomas, their respective birthdates were 1784 and 1796).

Daniel's grave was discovered by some workers clearing land on the very top of the hill where he lived. All gravestones lying flat on the ground.

After Michael and Catherine died, son John did not move over to his land along the river until 1882. Little wonder. He first had to clear 145 acres of virgin land, then build the house in which three generations of Beavers would live.

[After the last Beavers, Abe Beaver and his family, moved out of the old house, a series of tenants came and went. Might have lasted another century had it not caught fire and burned to the ground in the late nineteen-eighties.]

There has always been much speculation as to how John acquired that huge piece of property. Some say that he received it as a grant. Others, that he simply purchased it. His sketch merely states that he "located" there in 1882.

But own it he did, for on the map of Grandview Township in the *Atlas of Washington Co. Ohio 1875*, that huge tract of land is clearly labeled, "Jno Beaver."

It appears that Daniel's son (Daniel II) and his family also moved from Sheets Run over to Beavertown. During the oil boom of 1884, John became so busy tending his oil wells that he sold his store to cousin Daniel. He moved it down to the crossroads of Parr Hill and Old Beavertown Road.

Daniel III (Lyle Beaver's grandfather) took over after the death of his father. He married a McMasters girl who bore him four daughters— Grace, Hazel, Blanche and Ethel (Lyle's mother).

Nicknamed "Bub," he was a model citizen, even serving as chief law officer of Beavertown for a time. His store was doing well; he even had ten thousand dollars in the bank.

His wife died suddenly. He began to drink heavily. Lost his store with all its contents plus every cent of that ten thousand dollars. Ended up a bedraggled old man living with his new wife, Julia, and children in a shack with a dirt floor.

No information at all about Julia—Beavers just called her "Old Jude." She bore him at least two children—a son, "Jackalo" and a daughter, Jean ("Babe"). "Babe," stuck to her father like glue. Seldom saw one without the other.

"Jackalo" was married to a very pretty girl and lived near his father. They had two little girls and a cute little boy. Playing down in front of Beaver & Paynter's store one day, the poor little fellow ran out in front of a Greyhound bus and was killed.

Of course, like everyone else in Beavertown at that time, "Bub" was a big "moonshiner." In his spare time, made a tiny still for "Jude"—out of her snuff cans. Officers who discovered it were so impressed that they did not have the heart to destroy it. Took it along intact, and "even had it written up in the paper."

One tale about old Dan ("Bub") and his "moonshine" business must be "taken with a grain of salt," but here it is.

Some law man caught him digging a hole for a still. He claimed that he was just digging a hole in which to bury an old horse which he was about to "put down." They stayed right there until he killed the poor animal and buried it.

CHAPTER 4

y the time John Beaver and Daniel II moved over to his "145 acres of excellent land" along the Ohio River, he and Rebecca had thirteen children (eleven listed below):

William Columbus Beaver
Martha Beaver Northcraft
Isabelle Beaver Mounts
Jacob Elmer Beaver
Florence Beaver Mounts
Etta Beaver Thompson

Charles (Snapper) Beaver
Ada Beaver Lane
Harman Beaver
Elizabeth Beaver
Wesley (or Watson) Beaver

John's autobiographical sketch states that they had thirteen children, but only nine still living at the time. Below in its entirety:

John Beaver, one of the well-to-do farmers of Grandview township, Washington County, Ohio, is a native of Maryland where he was born May 16, 1831. He is the son of Michael and Catherine (Benine) Beaver. The latter is a native of Maryland, where she was born September 10, 1796.

Michael Beaver was a farmer all his life, and a valued member of his community. He was born in Germany, in 1784 and when still a youth he and his parents crossed the ocean to the United States and located, for the time, in Maryland.

In 1832 Michael Beaver left that state and settled in Monroe County, Ohio, where he bought his farm, and tilled the soil for many years. In 1838 he bought more property in Washington County, removed thither, and made his home there until his death.

Michael Beaver was united in marriage with Catherine Benine, and they reared nine children, three of whom now survive, namely: Nancy, who married Thomas Lee, and is a resident of Independence township; Rachel, who married Mr. Mount, and lives in Grandview township; and John.

John Beaver was reared and schooled in his native place. He has been a farmer all his life, and located on his present ample farm in 1882. It consists of 145 acres of excellent land, located in section 28, and well adapted to farming.

Mr. Beaver was united in marriage with Rebecca Thompson in 1856. She was a native of the Keystone State, and was born in 1840. They have thirteen children, nine of the family still living as follows: William, born January 13, 1858; Martha, born August 18, 1856, who married Mr. Northcraft; Belle, who was born June 29, 1860, and married a Mr. Mount; Elmer, born July 7, 1865; Florence, who married a Mr. Mounts; Etta, born June 29, 1871, who married Mr. Thompson of Marietta, Ohio; Charley, born August 26, 1875; Ada, who was born July 2, 1874, and married Harry Lane, and Harman, born August 13, 1881.

Mr. Beaver is a Democrat in political opinion.

Fraternally, he affiliated with J.O.U.A.M. He is a member of the United Brethren Church.

**Group picture of John's family and friends shows
John sitting at the center in the front row.**

Note that John devotes much of his sketch to his father, Michael — a "valued member of his community." The following entry in *Grandview Township's First Trustees Journal (1803-1843)* lends support to his statement:

> April 10, 1841. This day came Michael Beever and took the oath of office as fence viewer for Grandview Township. Recorded by me, Silas Ellis, T. Clerk. (Note first change in spelling of last name.)

A column written by Diana McMahan in the April, 2002 issue of *The Marietta Times*, contains this description of the office called fence viewer–

Fences were rare, for few families had time to build them. However, there was a township office called "Fence Viewer," an individual who checked the few miles of fences there were.

By the time John's sketch was published in 1902, he and his family had been living in the house which he had built, for twenty years. The house which three generations of Beavers would call home.

Although Beaver history can be traced back through the centuries, tons of research yielded little more about Rebecca than what John wrote in his sketch. Even genealogist Eileen Thomas was unable to find any more information about how and where the two happened to meet.

John's sketch states that Rebecca "was a native of the Keystone State," born there in 1840—although her tombstone bears the date of 1839.

Two views of "Dragon John's" tombstone up in Parr Hill Cemetery bearing the inscriptions: JOHN BEAVER MAY 1831–NOV. 21 1913 REBECCA HIS WIFE 1839–MAR. 8, 1911

(Another little oddity. That stone was set in backwards and never reset. (Eileen Thomas.)

The graveyard is about the only project in Beavertown which owes its existence to someone other than John Beaver.

Local school teacher, Henry Ellis, donated ground for the first section in 1850. Was also the first to be buried there two years later.

The other section was donated to the community by Albert and Ida Slack. Alma Slack Taylor (descendant of Rachel Beaver Mount) gave Mary Bradford this explanation of how that came about:

At the time of its inception the cemetery land was a pasture field. Alma's father, Albert, and his best friend Cliff Beaver were standing on the site one day and Cliff told Albert that he would like to be buried there. Within the year Mr. Beaver became ill and died. His good friend buried him there and donated the land for a cemetery. (Cliff Beaver was "Dragon John's" grandson.)

Different account from Eileen Thomas' complete history of Parr Hill Cemetery:

The old section of the cemetery is now called the Grandview Township Cemetery. Since reopening of the Parr Hill Church, the township has turned the responsibility of the cemetery back to the church.

Raymond "Doc" Beaver asked if Albert and Ida Slack would start a cemetery, and they agreed. Albert and Ida sold lots of four grave sites for $20 and eight for $40. Parr Hill acquired the middle section from Albert and Ida Slack. The Slacks would start at the other side of the first cemetery. At the gate—Ollie Beaver, ending with Clarence and Jack Cochran babies.

After the deaths of Albert and Ida, Arthur and Alma sold lots. After their deaths, Doyle Taylor sold some lots in the cemetery and two lots outside the fence to Elmer Bennett and Jeffrey Beaver.

The second section starts at Raymond "Doc" and Eunice Beaver and ends at Jack Haught. The third section starts at Maud and Cecil Beaver and ends at Bryan Beaver.

At the time of Eileen's writing, ninety-four Beavers had been buried in that cemetery.

Another tiny cemetery occupies one corner at the intersection of Parr Hill and Old Beavertown Roads. Revolutionary War soldier, Henry Franks, is buried there.

Hard to believe that one man (John) could be responsible for almost all of those buried upon that hill. But, he did build—and populate—one whole town all by himself. (With a bit of help from cousin Daniel.)

With his house under roof and family settled in, John moved a stone's throw to the right and began construction on the store which would serve the area for years.

Folks living in the area must have been delighted. Up to that time, only place to buy supplies was New Matamoras. Some six miles to the north. Over an unpaved road by horse and buggy. Ditto for mail.

CHAPTER 5

Once his store was under roof, John petitioned the state for a post office. Postal officials soon arrived to inspect the premises. Finding everything in order, they sat down to lay out terms and conditions.

Right off the bat, they hit a snag. Over of all things, the naming of the post office. What else but Beavertown Post Office? Not to be. Seems that there were "too many other places in Ohio with similar sounding names."

No record of proceedings exists, so no one knows how long it took to come up with an acceptable name. Today, the name on which they settled—Dawes—seems to have come straight out of "left field."

Not if one considers those times. In 1882, the Civil War still weighed heavily on the minds of Ohio Valley residents. Ohio had sent more of its young men off to battle than most other states.

Had any Beavers served the Union in that war? According to Kenneth Galbreath's list of those who served, four Beavers. One of whom—James Beaver—never came back.

James Beaver, age 19, volunteer, August, 1861 three years, Seventy-seventh regiment, Company C, private, served seven months, died fighting at Covington, Kentucky, in May of 1862.

Perry Beaver, age 23, volunteer, 1861, three years, Seventy-seventh regiment, Company C, private, served three years, mustered out December 12, 1864.

George W. Beaver, age 31, drafted and volunteer, 1862, three years, Seventy-seventh regiment, company C, private.

Michael Beaver, age 23, volunteer, November 1861, three years, Seventy-seventh regiment, company C, private, served two months, discharged.

Trouble was, all four bore the name Beaver. But—there was a general living down in Marietta. A much decorated general, Rufus R. Dawes.

A graduate of Marietta College, Dawes was in Wisconsin when President Lincoln issued his first call for troops. Rushing home, he assembled a company of volunteers and immediately reported for duty.

Histories of Washington County contain glowing reports about his leadership and courage. This excerpt from *Andrews History of Marietta and Washington County, Ohio*, describes his actions in the battle of Gettysburg:

At Gettysburg, his horse had been shot from under him, and he was unmounted. Climbing the fence, under fire with his regiment he charged the enemy. With one hundred eighty dead or wounded—out of the original four hundred twenty—Dawes, with a remnant of his regiment, reached the objective and received the surrender of the Second Mississippi Regiment.

The name, Dawes, evidently satisfied everyone, so Dawes it was. Beavers would pick up their mail at Dawes Post Office for the next thirty years. Maps of that time, labeled accordingly.

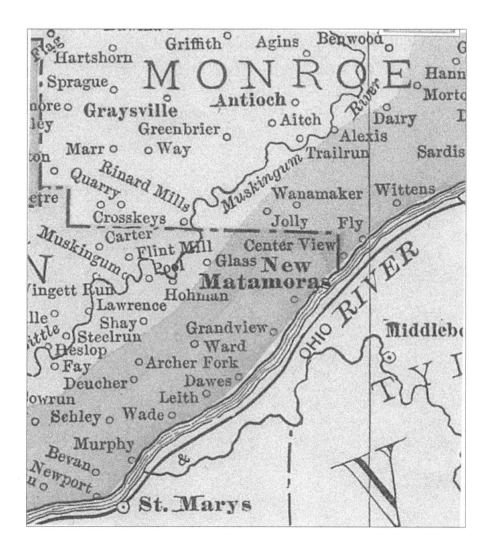

James Cochran was appointed first Post Master in 1882, followed by Daniel Webber in 1885. Succeeding postmasters — Samuel Cochran (1889); Setathiel Hutchison (1891); Aurelius Ellis (1893); William Beaver (1904) and Frederick Joy (1907). William Beaver served again until 1911, when Rural Free Delivery out of New Matamoras was established.

CHAPTER 6

*N*ame of the post office settled, John turned his attention to the river flowing right past his house. Unrestricted by dams, it wound lazily southward, with varying depths. (Depending on the amount of rainfall.) Except at flood times, folks could cross from the Ohio shore to West Virginia in a matter of minutes.

Eunice Beaver said that she used to "hike" up her long skirts and with kids in tow, step from sandbar to sandbar over to Bens Run. There was a tiny store there where she could purchase salt and a few other necessities.

Pollution free, the Ohio River then teemed with every sort of aquatic life. Especially mussels, which all but carpeted the river floor. Half shells of generations past littered the shores and turned up with every spring plowing.

Lined with iridescent mother of pearl, they could be used to make beautiful buttons. So button factories sprang up all along the river. Nearest to Beavertown, one down in St. Marys, West Virginia. That button industry would sustain Beavertown for almost two decades.

John boats and skiffs were of little use for mussel fishing. So John and the boys built special boats down on Jolly Landing.

[Jolly Landing was a stretch of sandy beach—beginning just below John's house and stretching downstream for almost half a mile. Special events like weddings and birthday parties were held there.]

Those mussel boats were strange looking contraptions—like something straight out of a Rube Goldberg cartoon. Very simple. Just long shallow wooden rectangles. A post at each end, upon which rested a pole equipped with several dangling iron hooks.

Mussel Fishing Boat

Out on the river, poles were lowered over the side. Hooks sank to the bottom; boats were then poled up and down the river. Hooks slipped right into opened mussel shells which clamped right on and never let go.

Loaded hooks were then yanked up, mussels pried off and tossed into the bottom of the boat. Once full, boats were poled to shore. Mussels dumped into huge iron pots of water heated to boiling over roaring wood fires.

Cooked mussels could then be easily picked out. Generally, by women and children who had to keep an eye out for an occasional pearl which might appear. Just as in oysters. Worth from one hundred to one hundred fifty dollars, pearls were made into rings, pins and tie tacks. Grandpa's old stick pin may well be sporting one of those old mussel pearls.

Mussel flesh, although quite tasty, was generally discarded. Empty shells were transported down river to the St. Marys button factory. For almost a decade, Beavertown (then known as Dawes) depended on mussel fishing for a living.

Lyle Beaver, who was old enough to be involved, said "Beavertown was one busy place in those days."

CHAPTER 7

$\mathcal{O}$nce the supply of mussels "fished out," Beavers could still depend on the river for sustenance. Built two packet boats—Beaver One and Beaver Two. These were used to transport goods and people up and down the river. Initially powered by wood burning boilers—later by gasoline. They remained in service well into the twenties.

One of two well known Beavertown boats (circa 1920), the Beaver No. 1. appeared in the 1998 Matamoras Historical Society calendar—month of March.

Standing on board the Beaver No. 1: Clifford Beaver, Howard Beaver and Charles (Link) Beaver—Lyle's stepfather. (Courtesy of the Lyle Beaver collection, Historical Society Museum)

Ninety-year-old Pearl Haught remembered those packets well. She and sister "Mickey" used to go over to the river to "flag down" a Beaver packet. Mostly to take a calf ready for butchering down to the stock market.

Packets were a huge improvement over the clumsy barges formerly used to move goods up and down the river. Going down to Marietta for supplies, a full day's journey. Horses had to be taken along to drag a barge over the sandbars and shallows. Then back upstream. Trips were few and far between.

With all of John's enterprises going strong, Beavertown was fairly prosperous. Then in 1884, the first oil well was drilled over in Macksburg, Ohio. From there, drillers moved around to the Ohio River and began drilling wells all along the river shore. Some of which, still pumping away.

Drillers soon reached John Beaver territory and drilled several wells there. Eunice said that folks around Beavertown were "green with envy." "That lucky dog. All he has to do is turn over a rock, and he'll find a pot of gold." That he did. Black gold.

Dawn to dusk—that was John's schedule. Since most of his oil wells were along the river, those sitting above on their porches watched him come draggin' along from one well to another, home about dark. They began calling him "Draggin' John." It stuck, and somewhere along the line would become "Dragon John." And thus he would be known for the rest of his life.

Eileen Thomas could not be sure just when Beavers began "all that nicknaming business." But touched on it in her internet notes, listing several which appear below:

Clyde Beaver	"Dude"	Willard Beaver	"Griz"
Oreton Beaver	"Booger"	Clarence Cochran	"Slopy"
Harmon Beaver	"Abe"	William Danver	"Cooney"
Veryl Beaver	"Cotton"	Ralph Cochran	"Drakey"
Cecil Beaver	"Blackie"	Charles Beaver	"Snapper"
Charles Beaver	"Link"	Ray Beaver	"Riddle"
Cecil Beaver	"Bull"	William Beaver	"Dapaw"
Earl Beaver	"Junky"	Raymond Beaver,	"Doc"
Raymond Beaver, Jr.	"Bugs"	Vernon Cochran	"Jiggs"
Vernon Beaver	"Johnny Boy"	Mabel Beaver Corum	"Jenny"

31

For many, many years, mail with nicknames was more apt to reach its destination than ones with given names.

No doubt John was aware of his nickname. Most of his contemporaries called him that. Not really suitable for one of the "well to do farmers of Grandview Township."

Lyle Beaver said, "John certainly did have money. Enough to give each of his children the choice of a plot of land or its equivalent in cash—five hundred dollars." A lot of money for that time. Only one daughter took the money and left.

John's granddaughter-in-law, Eunice, said that husband "Doc" used to come home with reports of seeing "wads" of money fall from behind pictures on the wall. When John died, neighbors said that his children went on a regular "treasure hunt" in and around his house. No reports of success or failure.

CHAPTER 8

All thoughts of John's money vanished with news of the government's plan to build a series of dams on the Ohio River. One of which—No. 16—would be built right in the center of Beavertown. Next four years would be some of the best Beavertown had ever seen.

By that time, all of John's children were married with children of their own. Oldest son William to Mary Butler of Wheeling, West Virginia; Charley to Molly Barker of Grandview, Ohio. Harman and Elmer also married (no names of spouses) and remained in Beavertown. One son, Wesley (or Watson) died in his teens of a shotgun blast to the stomach.

When John wrote his sketch, daughters, Martha, Ada, Etta, and Florence were all married. Martha—to James Northcraft over in Bens Run, West Virginia. Not far from home, for the river at that time could generally be crossed by just stepping from one sandbar to the other.

Etta married Mr. Thompson of Marietta, Ohio; Ada married Harry Lane. Florence married home towner A.M. Mount.

Isabelle (Belle) first married a Mr. Hutchison. When he died, she married John Mount who operated a store at the crossroads of Parr Hill and Old Beavertown Roads. Isabelle died in 1917.

When "Dragon John" died in 1913, eldest son, William Columbus, then became patriarch of Beavertown. Construction on the dam was in full swing, and everyone was busy and flush with money. William took full advantage. Built a new school house in the center of town and a new church house up on Parr Hill.

Those four good years soon passed, and hard times set in with a vengeance. Just when all seemed lost, Jacob Elmer discovered a way out. A most "unorthodox" way. He lived in a house just north of the junction of Parr Hill and Old Beavertown Roads. Most Beavers think that he was the first to make "moonshine" in Beavertown. Probably right.

Besides making "moonshine," Elmer was one busy man. Married twice—he sired four or five children with his first wife. Clyde "Dude," Glen, Nora and Della. Lyle thought one more boy, but could not remember his name.

"Dude" lived in Beavertown for much of his life. Had a beautiful bass voice. He and Ray (Riddle) Beaver and two "straight-laced" church ladies (twin sisters) were in great demand to sing at funerals. A balding, paunchy bass, a red-faced tenor with horn-rimmed glasses and two elderly widows dressed in all their finery.

Bass and tenor were often rumored to be "three sheets to the wind," but the ladies never seemed to notice. One son-in-law, who disliked his mother-in-law intensely, used to "needle" his wife about her "hypocrite of a mother standing up there singing with those two drunks."

Those widows surely did get around. Always had one or two old bachelors "on the string." No eHarmony in those days, but "lonely hearts clubs" abounded. Letters appearing in every magazine or newspaper.

If things got too boring, one of the ladies would invite a recent contact to come for a visit. He would be "wined and dined" long enough to keep the ladies happy, then sent away empty handed.

All of that singing at funerals would come to an end when "Dude" left for good.

Elmer's first wife died; and he remarried. A much younger lady named Etta _?_. One son was born to them, Elmer Jr. Elmer promptly put all of his property in his new son's name.

The child died shortly before his second birthday, and Elmer, not long after. With what folks called "questionable tactics" and the help of Elmer's sister, Daisy Sole, Etta managed to get the property transferred to herself.

Not long after, was in a car wreck, got a substantial settlement and moved away. (Lyle Beaver said, "Was never heard from again.") That property remained deserted until one of Elmer's descendants, Bill Beaver, decided to come back and build on it. Had to buy out sixteen heirs—only one signed for free.

[A little sidelight here. Recent oil and gas drilling in the Ohio Valley has brought names long forgotten to the fore. *The Marietta Times* has been full of legal notices by folks petitioning to have old oil leases set aside.

Among those petitions, one requesting that a lease owned by Elmer Beaver be vacated. So, Elmer's estate was never completely settled after all.]

Elmer's daughters—Della and Nora—never left Beavertown. Della married John Newlen who worked at Lock Sixteen. They lived in one of the two handsome brick houses built for the Lock Master and his assistant. One daughter, Esther Minger grew up there.

Lock Sixteen was one of the most beautiful along the Ohio River. The two brick residences sat a short distance apart on a little hill above Route Seven. In an age devoid of power-driven equipment, premises were kept immaculate. Not even a spear of grass allowed to escape.

On the riverside of Route Seven sat the brick lock house with all of its workings. Just below, a wide, wide concrete promenade. Until World War II, open to the public. Great place for roller skating, bike riding and gatherings of all kinds.

Once the writer and a couple friends actually dared to walk across the upper gate. Down the opposite side and back across the lower gate. Very foolhardy and dangerous. Whether from fright or reaction with the water, top layers of their hair actually stood on end during the entire walk. Never told their parents.

Watching boats "lock through" was a favorite pastime. Especially, excursion boats like the Gordon C. Green. Carloads of people from all over would drive down onto the promenade and park as close to the edge as possible.

"Well-heeled" passengers used to line up along the boat railing, exchanging greetings with those on shore. Some would toss handfuls of coins to the kids gathered there, creating a mad scramble to retrieve them.

Once water in the lock chamber was raised — or lowered — to the right level, the old boat would give one thunderous blast of its whistle. Enormous red paddle began churning up water, sending it off to the next lockage. Giving folks on shore this weird feeling that they were the ones moving instead of the boat.

With the bombing of Pearl Harbor, all frivolity came to a complete stop. Entire complex fenced in. KEEP OUT signs posted everywhere. No excursion boats, just LST's (Landing Ship Tanks) and other war vessels manufactured upstream. All headed for action on the high seas. Beavers would rush out on their porches to watch and wave to the sailors on board until they disappeared from sight.

When World War II was over, plans were made for a new set of dams on the Ohio. Spelling the end for those old dams. In March of 1975, Willow Island Dam became operative. Old Sixteen, abandoned, stood unused until sold and divided into lots.

Brick residences were also sold. Residents of one, John and Della Newlen, bought land down along the river and built a new house. Lived there until their deaths. Their daughter, Esther Minger, then lived there until her death.

Elmer's daughter, Nora, also remained in Beavertown all her life. She and her husband, Clyde Paynter, built a house on the very top of Parr Hill. Their children grew up there. Two girls, Ruth and Betty. One son, Bruce.

Ruth married a tall blond "bean pole" of a man who taught school in Matamoras for a time. They later moved away. As did Betty, who married Earl Williamson. Bruce also left Beavertown and never returned.

In the mid-twenties, a new highway was built parallel to the river, running right past the dam. Prior to that, John Mounts sold the store he operated, at Parr Hill and Old Beavertown Roads, to William Columbus and son, "Junky Earl." Built a new store a little north—just south of "Dragon John's" house. Turned out to be a great boon to business, for the new highway came practically to its edge. (Folks speculated he might have been privy to that information beforehand.) With his death in 1950, the store closed. Now a rental property.

Not so great for William and "Junky." When the road was finished, traffic by-passed their store entirely. All they could do was sit up there and watch as former customers passed them by.

Sometime later, "Junky" formed a new partnership with Clyde Paynter. Planted a peach orchard on top of Parr Hill, where Paynter lived, and built a grocery store down on the edge of Route Seven. High off the ground to avoid Ohio River flooding, that store, gasoline pumps, everything, sported Sterling gasoline's official color—apple green. Pictured, one of their advertisements given out to customers.

Some years, the river rose far above what they had expected. Everything in the store had to be moved to another location. Often, all the way down to "Snapper's" old dance hall at the lower end of Beavertown.

Sometimes even that was not out of flood's reach. One flood brought in a good sized paddle wheeler, leaving it high and dry on a slightly elevated place behind the dance hall.

In the early thirties, exceptionally high waters wrenched the huge Wheeling Tabernacle from its foundation and floated it downstream. Beaver men were seen rowing in and out as it drifted by, looking for anything worth salvaging. Never knew where it landed.

Over the years, flood waters brought a lot of salvageable materials. Drums of paint, varnish, oil—and lumber. Some claim that most Beaver houses were built with lumber brought down river by floods.

For kids, spring floods meant no school. Except for a few high spots, Route Seven was totally under water. For a brief period, the highway belonged to roller skaters and bike riders. When waters receded, there were piles of drift wood to be searched for hidden "treasures."

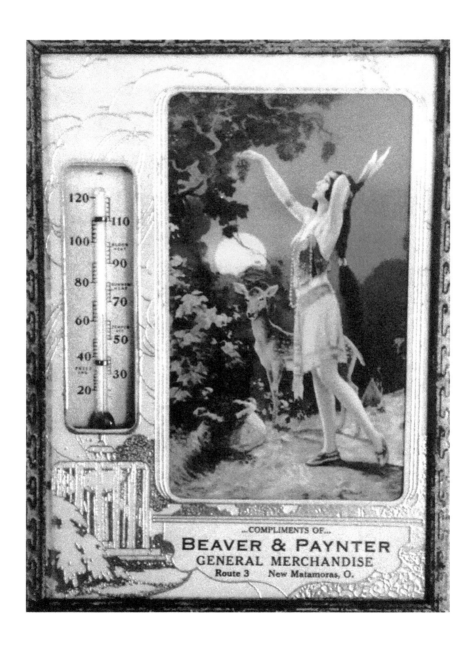

For adults, stuck with cleaning up, nothing but hard work. Every surface covered with slimy silt. No hoses or running water then. Just buckets and buckets carried from cisterns—pumped by hand. Little wonder that most Beaver houses were built high upon the hills, out of the reach of flood waters.

"Junky" and Paynter were about as mismatched as they come. "Junky" dressed like he was going to a funeral every single day. Always wore a white shirt. His salt and pepper hair closely clipped. A stub of cigar—seldom lit—between his teeth. Very business-like.

Lyle said "Junky' never 'dirtied his hands' making whiskey. But dealt in it and made a lot of money." He and his wife Blanche were divorced, but he stopped in to visit her every day.

"Paynter" was not much concerned with his appearance. Wearing ordinary working man's clothes, he greeted customers with a gold-toothy smile, surveying them over the top of steel-rimmed glasses. Wisps of thinning, graying hair left to wherever they would.

"Paynter" and "Junky" took turns running the store. Waiting on customers from behind a wide wooden counter which ran across the back of the store. Directly behind that counter, in the left-hand corner stood the huge round cheese table. Actually, a thick cross section slab sawn from an oak tree.

On top, wheels of various kinds of cheese, covered with cheese cloth. Using a big home-made butcher knife, whoever was minding the store would whack off a chunk of cheese where ever the customer indicated. Rip off a section of orangey-brown paper from its rack, wrap the cheese, tie it with a string hanging from the ceiling and pencil on the price.

Of particular interest to kids, the glass covered candy case on the left side of the store. So be-smudged by sticky fingers that one could hardly make out the contents. Stocked with all kinds of penny candy—jaw breakers, suckers (lollipops), licorice sticks—and heaven forbid—candy cigarettes. Also Mother Bakers Chocolate Squares (plain with no wrapping) for two cents. Not many takers.

Cases on each side of the counter framed a rectangular oiled black floor. Gathering place for men of the village. Sitting around on upended wooden cases and empty salt fish kegs, they discussed weather, latest news, almost everything. No fancy spittoons, just empty coffee cans for tobacco chewers.

Kids, on an errand for Mom, were subject to a little good-natured "razzing." Pearl and "Mickey" McPeek used to take eggs to the store to exchange for groceries. Always hoping for a few pennies left over for candy.

Pennies, or no, they seldom left empty handed. All they had to do was sing for the circle of men gathered there. Which, they reluctantly did. One of the men would "pass the hat," garnering a few pennies to pay for their candy.

That store was also the unofficial school bus stop for Beaver kids. Always a bumper crop, including the tearful first grader clinging to Mom's skirt. (No kindergartens then.)

"Paynter" would step in with a bit of sweet encouragement. Which the sniffling youngster took, and—coached by Mom—uttered a muffled "thank you" and boarded that big old yellow school bus.

But for that store, many families in the area would have gone to bed hungry. Almost everyone "ran a bill" and were very slow paying. Seldom, if ever, was any request to "put it on the bill" denied. Hard to tell how many dollars were left "on the books" when Gene Holdren bought the store in the 1950's.

CHAPTER 9

*M*ost colorful of John's children, Charles. (Aka "Snappin' Charlie," "Snapper," or "Pratt.") He was the most enterprising of them all. Suffered from a disease called St. Vitus's Dance. Characterized by muscular jerkings—particularly of the face and upper body. Never seemed to bother him, nor interfered with work or pleasure.

He married a stout little lady, Molly Barker, from Grandview, Ohio. They lived in Beavertown all their lives. Four children—Cecil ("Bull"), Ray ("Raybo"), Victor ("Vic") and Goldie.

When "Dragon John" died, everyone assumed that John's eldest son, William Columbus, would take command of Beavertown's affairs. Including getting ready for the new dam to be built right in the middle of town.

Instead, Charlie stepped right in. Immediately began preparations for workers who would be coming. On the right side of Parr Hill Road, overlooking the dam site, Charlie began work on the long two-story building which would house and feed all the workers who were bound to show up. And come they did. City slickers, backwoods men, "funny little foreigners," all their worldly goods wound up in red bandanas tied to sticks resting on their shoulders. Very young, but willing to work. (Sadly, two of them would never see home again.)

August 27, 1914, edition of the *Matamoras Enterprise* published this account of their demise:

TWO DROWNED

Dam No. 16 was the scene Thursday afternoon about 2:00 o'clock of a double drowning when two Italians who were employed on the work by Gillispie Company were bathing and got into a deep hole and before aid could reach them they drowned.

The names were George Corsi about 17 years old, and Bernardine Billie who was about 24 years old.

They came to this dam about 11 days before the accident and there is no way of finding out whether they have any relatives in the country or not.

The bodies were brought to R.M. Cunningham's undertaker's parlor Thursday afternoon about 7:00 and buried in the potter's field of Matamoras Cemetery.

Luckily, no Beaver lives were lost in the building of the dam. In fact, those days were some of the best Beavers had ever seen. Eileen Thomas, writing in her column for *Washington County, Ohio to 1980*, described it this way:

During the time the locks were building, Beavertown was a prosperous community. Dan Beaver had a grocery store, William Beaver ran a confectionary called "Pop's store." The Pete Dunn house was once a two-story home, which served as a restaurant, pool room, and boarding house. Earl ran the pool room in 1914–1916. John Mount had a grocery store, which Earl and his father, William, bought. These businesses were all located at the crossroads of Parr Hill and the Old Beavertown Roads.

Not only those looking for work headed for Beavertown. Just plain drifters found their way to Charlie's establishment. In keeping with its long-established tradition that "nobody ever came to Beavertown hungry and left hungry," he fed them all along with the locals.

Some came and never left. One entire family—blind man with wife and children—came and stayed until the very end. "Blind Tom" played the piano "like a pro" and Charlie was an expert accordionist. Evenings after supper, workers gathered around and were entertained royally until bedtime.

After four years of plenty, completion of the dam in 1917 found Beavers in relatively comfortable circumstances. However, clouds of war in Europe were threatening to engulf the United States. (Courtesy of the Matamoras Historical Society Calendar, a picture of Lock No. 16.)

Building Ohio River Lock No. 16, the Beavertown Dam, about 1918.

President Wilson managed to keep America out of the war until Germany announced unrestricted submarine warfare on the high seas. He then severed relations with that country. When German submarines actually began attacking American ships, that was the last straw. He declared war on April 6, 1917.

Congress passed the Selective Service Act, requiring all men between eighteen and thirty-one to register. Later, eighteen to forty-five. Ohio ended up putting 250,000 into service. Must have been some Beavers among them, although no Beaver names appear on Charles Galbreath's list of those killed in action.

No doubt that would have changed, had the war lasted longer. America's involvement began on April 6, 1917 and Armistice was signed on November 11, 1918.

With the signing of that armistice, the war on alcoholic beverages resumed in earnest. Prohibitionists had simply put their war "on the back burner" while the war was raging overseas. (Even at that, they managed to slip "a section prohibiting the manufacture of distilled liquor, beer and wine in the food control bill).

While Prohibitionists were much maligned for their actions—then and now—they were not completely out of line. Use of alcohol had become so pervasive that society as a whole was on the verge of breaking down. Women and children, in particular, paying a heavy price.

During the 1830's the average American was "downing" 90 bottles of eighty-proof whiskey per year. That included women—regular users of Lydia Pinkham's Vegetable Compound—21 percent alcohol.

Henry Howe, in his history of Ohio, put it this way:

Alcoholic beverages were considered a necessity of life; a sort of panacea for all ills, a crowning sheaf to all blessings, good in sickness and in health; good in summer to dispel the heat, and good in winter to dispel the cold; good to keep on work; and more than good to help on a frolic.

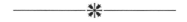

The state of Ohio became chief battleground for the fight against the sale of intoxicants, with women and clergy at the forefront. Anti-Saloon League was organized there, in 1893. Under its guidance—and persistence—individual states, one by one, went "dry."

In 1913 (the year in which construction on Lock 16 began), the League launched a national campaign for a Prohibition Amendment to the Constitution. After four more years, Congress finally provided for an amendment that would make the entire country prohibition territory. This was the Eighteenth Amendment—to take effect on January 16, 1920. It remained in effect exactly thirteen years, five months and nine days. To help enforce it, Congress passed the Volstead Act in 1919.

During that time, Beavers were so involved in the construction of the dam that they cared little about what was going on in the rest of the country. Work on the dam was still going on when President Wilson declared war on Germany. So they had little time to think about that war so far removed from their little town. By the time the war was over (was short, lasting only from April 1917–November 11, 1918), Beavertown was running out of money.

"Cotton" (William Columbus' grandson) put it this way, "We all knew about the illegal whiskey trade but never once considered going into it ourselves. The few samples we tasted were barely drinkable. We had no money to buy it anyway."

What "Cotton" didn't know—or anyone else—Uncle Elmer Beaver had slipped around and set up a still on the sly. Must have been at it for quite a while, judging by the kegs of gold coins hidden in his bedroom.

Only one person was allowed to enter that bedroom, daughter-in-law Leila. Whether she "let the cat out of the bag" or someone just stumbled onto his secret, no one knows. However, stills began popping up like mushrooms in every nook and cranny—and never stopped for thirteen years. "Cotton" said, "It happened almost overnight. No cooperation, no order. It all just 'kina' happened."

At what point Charlie joined the others is not clear. Business man that he was, spent some time assessing the situation, before actually setting up his operation.

Began by buying a big house some distance to the south of Beavertown proper. Big enough for his growing family and a good-sized whiskey operation. Sold an enormous amount of "moonshine" from there all through Prohibition times.

He and wife Molly moved in and raised four children there. Along with caring for four children, Molly also served as Charlie's "right hand man." Her specialty, aging "green" whiskey.

Any type of motion will hasten the process. Her favorite method—a five-gallon keg of "green" whiskey secured beneath her skirted rocker. Aged gallons of whiskey while rocking her babies to sleep (not the only skirted rocker in Beavertown).

Larger batches were aged in fifty-two gallon barrels out in Charlie's store room. Purchased from a supplier in Canton, Ohio, they came already charred on the inside. Most of Beavertown's supplies came from that city.

Holes (called bung holes) were drilled into the side of each barrel (which held fifty-two gallons). Plugs (bungs) were fashioned to fit snugly into those holes. Barrels had to be turned frequently, bung removed, and contents tested for readiness. Three months produced a good product, but the longer, the better.

Initially, testing was done by just tasting. However, before it was over, most "moonshiners" had managed to acquire genuine government testers. Charlie's daughter-in-law thought "there might still be one around there someplace." Turning and testing those barrels kept Charlie busy. However, he did have a helper. A most unusual helper.

In those days, it was quite common for folks to take in wild "critters" for pets. A family who lived just north of Beavertown had a pet raccoon. The Hutchisons used to stop there just to watch it eat. Every raccoon, if water is available, washes its food carefully before ingesting it. (World Book Encyclopedia.)

Two wild squirrels—orphaned by some hunter's bullet—were adopted by the Hutchison family. Grew rapidly and were given the run of the house. Until one day they discovered some toothache pills in the kitchen cupboard. Ate them, and died.

Charlie had a pet crow. A regular nuisance, a pesky bunch of feathers with an eye for anything shiny—earrings, cuff links and the like. An inveterate trickster, never missed a chance to yank the mosquito netting off the sleeping baby.

One day, the old bird found Charlie's store room door ajar. Flew up and landed on one of those barrels. Nothing of interest there except those plugs sticking up out of each barrel. Began pecking away at the plug until it came loose and fell off onto the floor.

Faced with that open hole, the old bird stuck its bill right down into the contents. Took a sip and blinked a few times. Took another. Then another. Finally, too drunk to maintain its perch, fell off onto the floor. Lay there in a mound of limp feathers, where Charlie found it.

Thinking that it was probably a "goner," picked it up and took it into the house. Surprisingly, it survived. Not only survived, but at every opportunity, would sneak back into that barrel room and "get smashed" all over again.

Both of Charlie's sons married and remained in Beavertown for much of their lives. Cecil had the misfortune to be caught in the very act of making whiskey (with Matamoras Dr. Rowles looking on). Was arrested and carted off to jail in Marietta. Lyle Beaver said "Someone higher up managed to get him off. He left town and went to Florida until things cooled off."

Ray married Dorthy Wright (Martin Wright's daughter). They lived up on Old Beavertown Road. When Dorthy's parents passed away, moved down into their house.

In the 1940's Charlie's old "moonshine" house came up for sale. "Raybo" and Dorthy bought it, moved in and lived there the rest of their lives.

This writer spent many happy times with Dorthy and daughter Shelda. Lots of what is written here comes straight out of those times. A good example.

Ray and Mart were operating a still right across Route Seven from Mart's house. Down under the riverbank. Stills were always in danger of blowing up, so had to be watched carefully. Mart and Ray were taking turns watching it.

Ray had just relieved Mart and was sitting there whittling away on a stick when he heard a twig snap. Looked up straight into a barrel of a law man's gun. Almost without thinking, Raybo charged the guy, knocked him over the bank and took off.

Running across the highway to the house, he told Dorthy to throw some clothes into a bag. "We're leaving!" Headed for sister Goldie's house in Zanesville, Ohio. Stayed there until they thought it was safe to come home.

Ironically, they later learned that law enforcement was, at that very time, setting up regional headquarters in Zanesville. Gearing up for the final battle to stamp out "moonshine" making in the area once and for all.

Meanwhile, back in Beavertown, the lawman—bleeding profusely from Ray's knife wound—headed for the nearest house. (Which just happened to belong to Dorthy's Aunt Maggie.) Maggie bandaged his wound the best she could, dodging his questions all the while.

One of Ray and Dorthy's best customers was their family doctor. (Actually, doctor to all of Beavertown.) He liked his whiskey colored like commercial brands. Every now and then, he would bring them a fresh supply of coloring. Says a lot about the safety of Beavertown whiskey.

"Hot toddies," (a mixture of whiskey, sugar, nutmeg and a little hot water) taken at bedtime was a main stay. "Would sweat a cold right out of a person." If nothing else, guaranteed a good night's sleep.

Grandma Belle Hutchison always kept a bottle of "camphorized" whiskey on hand. Made by shaving a cake of camphor into a pint bottle of "white lightning." Good for almost all ailments. A sniff or two for a "stopped up" head. A rub for that pesky "rheumatiz." Colicky babies? This formula (actually doctor approved):

One ounce warm water
¼ teaspoon sugar
15–20 drops of whiskey

While Beavertown was mainly known for its whiskey, beer ("home brew") was generally preferred by most locals. Had to be made "on the sly" since all alcoholic beverages were illegal.

With the area practically floating in whiskey, not much use trying to make one's own. Beer, an entirely different matter. Almost everyone made "home brew."

That "home brew" was wonderful. Nothing like commercial brands. Ingredients—just a can of Blue Ribbon malt (available at almost any store), yeast, sugar and water. Mixed up and allowed to work for a period of time. Maybe a week or more. Bottled and stored away in a cool place.

Here is how bottling went at the Hutchison house. In a secluded place away from prying eyes, salvaged ketchup or beer bottles were cleaned thoroughly with a mixture of sand and water. Filled with new beer and capped with the old ketchup bottle capper.

After dark, Dad and girls carried it all over to the root cellar and stored it in with the cans of fruit and vegetables. Dad snapped the padlock on the hinge flap and pocketed the key. "Now, you girls don't go 'messin' around over here or go 'blabbin' about it all over."

They waited patiently until they were certain the beer was ready. Catching Dad over in the field planting corn one day, they decided to "sneak over" and taste some of their wares.

Gathering up key, flashlight (cellar was dark), dishpan and bottle opener, they hurried over to the cellar. If not opened very carefully, "home brew" had a way of bursting from the bottle and shooting straight up in the air. Hence the dishpan.

One held the flashlight and the dishpan while the other slowly pried the cap off. Straight up into the air it went. Pan holder was able to catch but little of the contents. They "downed" it hurriedly, gathered up their equipment and took off.

Never again. Hardly worth the razor strapping they would get if Dad found out. Dad was still plowing away, thank goodness. Hurrying back to the house, they put everything back where they found them. Breathing a sigh of relief, took off for the barn to play with the cats.

Some days later, Mom and younger daughter went to a church meeting. Dad took the elder daughter over to the local restaurant for a little refreshment and to chat with some of the "regulars" gathered there.

Sitting around one of the larger tables, several acquaintances were discussing events of the day. Various topics, but generally gripes about Prohibition.

"I don't really miss all that whiskey much," said one. "But I sure do miss my beer." All nodded in unison. "Yeah, I could sure go for a bottle of that good old Iron City right now," said one. Others followed with their own favorite brands.

From back in one corner, on Dad's lap, came this little testimonial, "I like the kind Daddy makes best." Dead silence. Then everyone burst out laughing.

Although Beavertown was known mainly for whiskey, there were a lot of beer makers. One day, word of a raid came to one family who had just finished bottling a huge batch of beer. Springing into action, they carried every bottle over to a field nearby. Hid it in the tall grass, then came back to the porch and sat down to wait.

Time passed, and nothing. The sun rose higher and higher and the bottles began to pop. First one, and then another, until a steady pippity-pop filled the air. Then, dead silence. What a waste! All they could do was round up supplies for another batch and start over.

CHAPTER 10

efore whiskey days, Beavers made a living in various ways. Some quite unique. Dorthy Beaver's Grandma Lee and her husband (reputed to be a "dark man") lived on a house boat.

Rowing a skiff, her husband would tow the boat down to the Fenton Glass Factory in Williamstown, West Virginia. Loaded up with dishes and began the slow, slow journey back up river, peddling dishes at every little town and village along the way.

On reaching Wheeling, crossed over to the other side of the river and let the current carry them back to Williamstown to reload. Some of those old Fenton pieces bringing fabulous prices may well have come from Grandma Lee's houseboat.

During depression years, houseboats were familiar sights, but unlike Grandma Lee's boat, most were stationary. Just a few yards north of the Beavertown sign, sat one of those houseboats firmly anchored to the shore.

Houseboat

A Howell family lived there—father, mother and one son Lon. Only way to get aboard was over a narrow gangplank. Even when the river was calm, crossing that gangplank was pretty scary. If a paddle wheeler had just gone by, impossible.

Bigger the steam boat, more violent the rocking. Excursion boats like the Gordon C. Green threatened to tear the old houseboat completely off its moorings.

Across Route Seven from that houseboat lived the Hutchison family. Dad, Mom and two little girls—about four or five. That houseboat had given them many a scary ride over the years.

Hearing the blast of its foghorn whistle down at Lock Sixteen, they dropped everything. Raced down the hill, across the highway and down over the narrow gangplank. Boarding just as the huge boat came into view.

For a good fifteen minutes or more, everything on board rattled and shook, while those inside "held on for dear life." Sounds pretty tame today. But in those days, entertainment was wherever one found it—or made it.

Mr. Hutchison and the Howell son, Lon, used to play checkers in the evening by the flickering light of an oil lamp. On a square section of wood with squares penciled in. "Men" were just red and yellow grains of corn. Two grains for a king.

A few feet to the south stood a sign—BEAVERTOWN UNINCORPORATED, which marked the entrance to "moonshine" country. From there on, about three miles or so of nothing except Beaver houses—and Lock Sixteen.

A few steps beyond that sign, sat a house belonging to Ray "Riddle" Beaver and wife Martha.

"Riddle," "Slopy" Cochran and "Cotton" Beaver were among the first to enter the "moonshine" market. "Cotton" was only nine years old at the time. Unusual, for most Beaver children were not involved in the "moonshine" business at all.

A bit north of Riddle's house sat the old McMahan house. Unoccupied for years, it was barely livable, but the only available house which the Hutchisons could find to rent.

Never would they have ended up in whiskey territory but for the crash of 1929. Mr. Hutchison went to work one day and found the steel mill in which he had been working locked up tight. All they could do was pack up and head for home, back to the Ohio Valley where they had both grown up.

Actually, the old house was just a shell in which no one had lived for years. No utilities at all. Heating and cooking both by wood. Kerosene lamps for lighting; wash water caught in a rain barrel. (Generally inhabited by "wiggle tails"—mosquito larvae—which the girls spent hours watching.)

Although on the very edge of infamous Beavertown, it was quite peaceful there. For that matter, Beavertown itself was generally quite peaceful. Sometimes the girls would wander off a bit. Came back with tales about seeing "men filling jugs with something." Mom just said, "Nothing to worry about. They were just running whiskey."

Although not much of a "drinker," Dad actually found living so close to all that whiskey rather comforting. On occasion, taking the girls along, he would drive the old Whippet down Ohio Seven and stop at this big white house on the hill.

Lady of the house sold whiskey by the "shot" right there on her kitchen table. When she poured Dad's drink, always poured a little shot glass of seltzer water for each of the girls. Amazed the girls by wallowing a honey bee to death in the sand with her big bare toe.

No problem taking the girls along for the ride. They were as safe in Beavertown as their own house. But there were other dangers of a different kind. Making "moonshine" was not the safest occupation in the world.

A bit south of the Hutchison house sat a little bungalow on the river bank. Home to Charlie's son "Vick," wife Jessie and their small baby.

One day "Vick" put a batch of whiskey on the kitchen stove, then left on a short errand. A breeze blew the kitchen curtain onto the flame, catching fire. Soon the whole kitchen was ablaze. Jessie grabbed the baby, took her outside, laid her on a blanket and went for help. By the time she returned, the fire had consumed the house, the bushes around it and the poor little infant.

Trouble seemed to follow "Vick" around. Mainly having to do with whiskey business. Caught in the very act of running a still, he bolted and ran. Lawmen finger printed the still and went looking for him. By the time they caught up with him, he had sandpapered his fingertips, making identification impossible. So he "got off."

Charlie's boys looked so much alike that—especially from a distance—law men could hardly tell them apart. The boys took full advantage—cutting and combing their hair the same way. Also, wearing much the same clothing. Lawmen could never be sure just which Beaver they were chasing.

Daughter Goldie married a man named Sam (last name unknown). Actually lived in Zanesville, Ohio, but spent much of their time in Beavertown. No children. Traveled around in a little black coupe with a rumble seat.

Goldie surveyed the world through glasses with triple, triple thick lenses. Bronzy-gold hair bobbed and permed in twenties style, she wobbled around unsteadily on super high heels. Creating the impression that she had been nipping at some of her father's wares.

By this time, Prohibition was over. Her father's wares now quite legitimate. At Prohibition's end, he had sold his house in Beavertown and purchased a huge tract of land down on Route Seven. Partnering with Bryan Beaver (who dropped out later), built a two-story building. Tavern on the ground floor, living quarters on the second.

A few yards away, a two-stall "privy." One section marked WOMEN, the other, MEN. Tavern and "privy" all painted bright orange.

[W.A. Heiney's son, Donald, operated a gas station there until his death.]

Entering by the front door (facing the highway), stood the long shiny bar with high bar stools. Space behind filled with tobacco products (Mail Pouch for chewers. Bugel for rolling cigarettes). Also, all kinds of gum (Juicy Fruit, Beemans, etc.).

On the right, a juke box seldom silent. Right next to that began a row of wooden booths which ran all along the opposite wall.

Both Molly and Charlie tended bar, but they also hired full time help, Pearl Wright (Dorthy Beaver's sister). Dumpy little Molly, wearing a white bib apron over her print dress, filled in as needed. Wearing carpet slippers which had seen better days, she waited on customers, shuffling back and forth between bar and booths.

Charlie, or "Snapper," as he was mainly known then, hovered around the premises, shrugging and jerking all the while. Folks were often heard wondering if "he might not be putting it on a bit."

Most of the time, the place was fairly peaceful. Customers were mostly locals, not likely to cause trouble. Although "Snapper" was said to have carried a small "black jack" in a side pocket, just in case. No one ever really saw it.

Charlie died in 1949, (at age sixty-nine). Molly closed the place for good. Had a small room built onto the kitchen where she spent most of her time. Not long after, sold the whole place to W.A. Heiney who had been transferred from the Apple Grove locks to Lock Sixteen.

She then built a little white house just across the highway from the "beer joint." Spent the rest of her life there. That house is long gone, now replaced by a sales lot for used heavy equipment and replacement parts.

Beavers were still in the "moonshine" business when the depression hit and had yet to feel the full impact. So when the Hutchisons hit Beavertown, and moved into the house with no utilities at all, they had to get rid of some of their modern conveniences. Sold almost everything to Beavers who evidently were still flush with whiskey money.

Fortunately, they were able to keep their brand new Whippet. (Most popular automobile of the time.) Bought and paid for just before the "crash." An investment which would end up paying for itself many times over.

Barely settled, they learned that Matamoras School District was looking for someone to transport a few students to the high school in Matamoras. All that was needed was a chauffeur's license and a good car. Mr. Hutchison applied and got the job.

Could not have been a better fit. Having grown up on Sheets Run, Mr. Hutchison knew the area well. Although it was one of the toughest, roughest routes in the school system. Just sand and gravel—and very often, just plain mud. Never easy, even in good weather, but in winter nigh impossible.

No anti-freeze then, so the car radiator had to be drained every night. It was up at the crack of dawn every morning, stir up the fire in the old pot-bellied stove and put on a tea kettle of water. Once heated to boiling, it was carried down to the barn to refill the radiator.

No automatic starters, just cranking. Success rarely on the first turn. Not only that, cranks often "kicked back," delivering a painful blow to hand or arm.

In winter, chains on tires—absolute necessity. Much of the time, wheels would be hub-deep in mud or snow. Kids who lived on the Run had to walk to school. Some for three or four miles. After dropping the town students at the one-room schoolhouse, he would often drive back and pick up a load of walkers and deliver them to the school house.

With the coming of summer, things got much better. Although wood still had to be cut for the cook stove, pastures "brushed" with a man powered scythe. But a welcome change in diet. Fresh fish swimming around in a wash tub on the back porch. (Caught by the dozens in an illegal chicken wire trap.)

Greens of all kinds—dandelion, wild lettuce, water cress, etc. Later, young poke and milk weed. Cooked like spinach and served hot with vinegar dressing. Welcome change from winter's sauerkraut.

Come planting time, Uncle "Billow" Flowers came down from Matamoras with his team of horses to plow the garden. One day, his plow "resurrected" a keg of Beavertown "spirits." His blue eyes lit up, and he stopped dead in his tracks.

Whistling through his gold teeth, hurriedly switched the horses from plow back to wagon. Loaded the keg aboard and covered it with hay. Slapped the horses across their rumps with the reins and took off. Still whistling as he disappeared over a rise in the road.

CHAPTER 11

*S*uddenly life for the Hutchisons took a turn for the better. Mr. Hutchison was offered a job managing a huge farm down on the lower edge of Beavertown.

Owned by the Miracle family up in Matamoras, the farm boasted an almost new house, with not only electricity, but free gas. Plenty of water from a pump close at hand. Plus the unheard salary of one whole dollar a day!

First to be moved out of storage, Mom's prized KITCHEN QUEEN cook stove which she had not been able to part with. (Lit with just a match and a turn of a knob.) Old kerosene lamps were just left behind. Electrified lamps which had been carefully wrapped, along with the elephant lamp with beaded shade, all brought out and plugged in.

Along with all those blessings, came company. Lots of company. Relatives from both sides of the family. Former city friends, eager to partake of all the good things which farms have to offer. (Not to mention all that wonderful "moonshine"— right next door.)

However, if they expected to find whiskey in the Hutchison house, they were sadly disappointed. Outside, another matter entirely. Corn was not the only thing to be found in the old corn crib. Generally, the last stop on a guided tour around the farm.

Wanted or not, the girls (about five and six by then) usually tagged along on almost every trip. Alert for anything that "Mom ought to know about." Fascinating, how those men could hoist that stone jug over one shoulder, turn their mouths to the opening and drink.

Try as they might, the girls were never able to master that maneuver. Using vinegar jugs of water, ended up soaking wet time after time. Evidently, those men must have been practicing a lot.

Most puzzling of all. After a couple "good swigs," those men would make the "horriblest" faces followed by loud "whew-ees!" If the stuff was that bad, why in the world would they want to drink it in the first place?

A couple uncles—one from each side of the family—were real problems. One day they just disappeared and never returned, even for supper. Dad went looking for them. Hearing voices coming from the old red barn, he opened the door and slipped in.

Standing there in a barrel of Red Dog (floury substance made to be mixed with water and fed to the hogs) stood one uncle. Preaching to the other who was just sitting there, bleary eyed, on a bale of hay.

Strange, the way alcohol seems to bring out religion in many who over indulge. Local bartenders claim that they hear about as many hymns in their establishments as they would in church.

Just as the Hutchisons were settled comfortably in their new home and Mrs. Hutchison was finally adjusting to living in the heart of "moonshine" country, tragedy struck.

Mr. Hutchison was helping brother Bob butcher a couple pigs. Rifle used to kill the pigs was left leaning against the barn. Someone stumbled over it, causing it to go off. Sending a bullet right into the group of men working on the pigs.

Struck Mr. Hutchison in the knee. He was rushed to Marietta Hospital, treated, released shortly and sent home with the bullet in his knee. He did recover, but in caring for him his wife caught a cold which developed into pneumonia.

She never recovered. Died at the mere age of thirty-two, leaving Mr. Hutchison to raise the two girls alone.

With the help of a hired housekeeper, he stayed on, and managed to keep things going, though his leg stayed bluish-red and swollen tight.

Unbelievably—more bad luck. Again, involving guns and alcohol. Not long after, he and some friends were shooting rats up around the pig pen. Perched on the wooden gate, one shooter (who just happened to be his future father-in-law) fell off. His shotgun discharged, sending the full charge into Mr. Hutchison's wounded leg.

No E-squads then. Just a wild ride, some ninety miles an hour, down Route Seven to Marietta Memorial Hospital. He survived—only because brother Oza had the presence of mind to keep a tourniquet on that leg all the way to the hospital.

But there was no saving the leg this time. He would walk with an artificial leg for the rest of his life. Maintaining the farm was now out. He and the girls moved down to Uncle Oza's and lived there for some time.

About a year later, he met and married a young lady who lived next door. They rented a house up in the center of Beavertown. A house which "Lyle and others" had caught in the flood. No "moonshine" money there then, just some very, very hard times.

CHAPTER 12

*E*lection of Franklin Roosevelt finally brought some hope to Beavertown. Which came in the form of canned fruit, bags of raisins, nuts, etc. Sent home with school children. Later, free clothing and bedding—made by government sponsored "sewing room ladies" working on the top floor of the Matamoras Elementary School house.

Those ladies also turned out hundreds of shirts and dresses, all off the same pattern. With only slight variation of pattern and material. Although much appreciated, signaled to the rest of the community who was poor enough to be "on relief." (Today, known as welfare.)

Needless to say, much of what those ladies made ended up in Beavertown. Not unusual to meet someone else wearing the identical shirt or dress.

Some programs were mainly established just to "help the esprit de corp of the rural people and provide jobs for some of them." One of those programs was set up at Lock 16 in Beavertown, Ohio. Women from as far away as Matamoras and Wade met every week or two. A teacher came and taught them how to mold clay, paint, use glazes and create art forms.

Of those who participated—Virginia Beare, Maud Cochran, Iva Deshler, Margaret McMahan, Ethel May Noland, and Minnie Smurr. All ladies of some standing in the area.

Samples of that pottery can still be found in hands of local collectors. On display at the Matamoras Public Library in December of 2000. (*Muskingum Valley Review, December 10,* 2000.)

Although held in Beavertown, no Beaver women were included. Perhaps not considered "sophisticated" enough for such an undertaking. Most of those listed above had little or no connection to Beavertown.

For Beavers radios were the mainstay of morale. Never missed Roosevelt's "fireside chats." Comedies like "Lum and Abner," "Amos and Andy" and Jack Benny to keep spirits up.

Unfortunately, from those same radios came news not so uplifting. The war in Europe was threatening to draw America in. Then, suddenly, on December 7, 1941, the country of Japan conducted a sneak attack on Pearl Harbor.

Along with the rest of the country, Beavertown geared up for action. Several young men enlisted immediately. Entire Beaver families migrated to the big cities to work in factories making war material. Among them, the Hutchison family—to Akron, Ohio.

CHAPTER 13

$\mathcal{T}$hus far, this history has dealt with only two of "Dragon John's" sons–Jacob Elmer and Charlie. Information about youngest son, Harman, very, very sketchy. Although he was just as much involved in the "moonshine" business as the others. May be because he lived so far away from the main body of Beavers.

He and his wife, Fannie, lived in "Dragon John's" old house. Situated on the far north end of Beavertown. They raised seven children there. Eight, counting adopted son, Dewey ("Deacon") Moore. All eight, listed below:

Norman (Gus)	Harman (Abe)
Edna Beaver Cecil	George (Jumbo)
Ornton (Booger)	Lex
Thelma (Bunt) Carpenter	Dewey (Deacon) Moore

Very little is known about Harman's "moonshine" business. However, everyone seemed to know about this one incident involving one daughter's system of "delivering the goods."

During Prohibition times, most men wore high top shoes or boots. Flat pint-sized bottles of whiskey could easily be slipped down inside and carried around from place to place with no one the wiser. (Hence the term, "bootleg whiskey.")

Harman's daughter simply adapted that practice to her own purpose. Sewed pockets to fit pint bottles into the lining of her big fur coat, then tucked a pint of whiskey into each. Boarded the Greyhound Bus and delivered goods to clients all over the valley.

Probably never fooled anyone — including the driver. At that time, everyone and everything coming out of Beavertown was automatically suspect.

CHAPTER 14

$\mathcal{B}$orn January 13, 1858, "Dragon John's" eldest, William Columbus, was a force to be reckoned with. Also known as "Bill" or "Dapaw," he sired twelve children who turned out to be the whiskey generation. All twelve listed below, along with group picture.:

Fred Beaver
Daisy Beaver Sole
Ollie Beaver Beaver
Pearl Hattie Beaver
Sylvia Beaver Abbot Beaver
Willard Beaver

Earle Beaver
Dorthea Mae Beaver
Raymond Ray Beaver
Icy Vera Beaver Cochran
Roy Beaver
Clifford Beaver

**Front row sitting, left to right: Ollie Beaver Beaver;
William Columbus; Daisy Beaver Sole; Sylvia Beaver Abbot.
Standing, left to right: Icy Beaver Cochran; Fred Beaver; Roy Beaver; Willard
(Griz) Beaver; Raymond (Doc) Beaver; Earle (Junkey) Beaver.**

William and his father had practically nothing in common. In today's world, "Dragon John" would be considered a "workaholic." Not William. He preferred a more "genteel" way of making a living.

Grandson "Cotton," called him a horse trader, a wheeler-dealer, a "huckster." Always looking for a better or easier way of doing things. He "kept his finger on everyone's pulse," and brooked little nonsense from anyone in his town.

Not much happened in Beavertown without his "say-so." Under his watchful eye, life in Beavertown was generally calm and orderly. Daughter-in-law Eunice remembered it with fondness:

There was no going out of town for groceries. We made practically everything ourselves. Flour we got by grinding wheat, buckwheat or corn.

We butchered our own hogs and put the meat down in brine for six weeks, then laid it out on a board to let it "dreen." Then we hung it out in the smoke house to be sliced off as needed. It would keep forever.

Everybody kept a barrel of molasses for sweetening.

When folks got lonely or depressed, one neighbor would announce a "get together." Would last all day. There was lots to eat–with evenings reserved for "taffy pulls." Nights for dancing.

Sounds idyllic, and William Columbus intended to keep it that way—with a few improvements. Not long after "Dragon John" died, William decided that the town really needed a saloon. A place where men could go, have a drink or two and "chew the fat" without any interruptions from "women folk."

He built the saloon right across from his house and was soon doing a thriving business. Until one night he was awakened by shouts of "Fire! Fire!" Before anyone could lift a finger, the saloon had burned to the ground.

There was evidence of arson, but no one could say for sure who the "fire bug" might have been. Chief suspect, old Aunt Hannah Beaver (Joe Beaver's mother). Her husband had been spending an awful lot of time there. "But nothing ever came of it." (Lyle)

William also took over his father's packet boat business. From the files of Eileen Thomas, this bit of information about those boats:

WILLIAM BEAVERS BOATS

There were other boats in addition to the mussel boat fleet. The Beaver family had prospered and they owned at least two packet boats on the Ohio River.

These boats were named Beaver No. 1 and Beaver No. 2. They seemed to be a community project, both in ownership and the crew who worked on them. Earl Beaver was the pilot on No. 2. The Beaver No. 1 sank above Lock 16 before No. 2 was built.

Dates for these two are not presently known. However, the Matamoras Enterprise, dated December 17, 1914, has a note under the Sheets Run items: "Beaver No. 2 is going to run an excursion to Marietta this week. Now is the time to do your Christmas shopping."

A copy of the Matamoras newspaper, THE WEEKLY MAIL, of November 8, 1889 gave this account: Boats were the major means of transportation in 1889 and were always featured in the news.

The tow, Beaver, sank a barge of coal in the lower end of town last week.

When "Dragon John" died in 1913, William Columbus took over running the boat business. More than likely, wrote the above notice himself.

Best known of his projects (and there were several) his legendary "Pop Shop." A confectionary built at the wooden bridge marking the intersection of Parr Hill and Old Beavertown Roads. He could not have chosen a better time. Dam Sixteen was under construction; everyone was working and had money in their pockets.

He sold all kinds of sweet treats, but ice cream cones were his specialty. (To quote Lyle, "A four-inch cone with about a tablespoon of ice cream for a penny.")

Ice cream itself was hardly new, but ice cream cones did not appear until 1904 at the Louisiana Purchase Exposition in St. Louis. Their popularity spread rapidly to almost every part of the country.

In rural Beavertown, ingredients — milk, eggs, sweetener (molasses) — were plentiful. Salt required for the freezing process readily available across the river in the little Bens Run store for just a few cents.

What about the ice? Took lots and lots of ice. Where was he going to get that? No problem. In those days, the Ohio River was always frozen solid all winter, shore to shore. In the preceding winter, William just hitched old "Dobbin" to the sled and drove right out onto the glassy surface.

Put men and boys to work cutting and sawing out blocks of ice. Loaded them onto the sled. Hauled it all up the bank to be stored in sawdust beneath his shop.

There they remained, solid as a rock, until time to make his ice cream.

Making ice cream is not easy even now. Ice cream freezers had to be cranked by hand. Not William's "cup of tea." He hired Lyle and George Beaver (boys of about ten and twelve) for the summer. Taking turns at the crank, they managed to keep going to the end.

Lyle laughed wryly, "Well, the pay was pretty good. We got to lick the paddles when they were pulled out of the frozen ice cream."

Keeping an eye on everything and everyone in Beavertown kept William busy. So busy that he completely missed the "moonshine" operation right next door. Run by none other than his own son and daughter-in-law, "Doc" and Eunice. How in the world did he miss that?

"Well, we were extremely careful," said Eunice. "Never, never sold from our house and chose our buyers carefully. We also had a friend high up in the law business—the county sheriff himself. We were the only ones never hauled into court."

Why did they not want William Columbus to know? Because of religion?

"Hah!" snorted Eunice. "That old man never set foot in a church house in his life. But he made sure everyone else did."

Even had a brand new church house built up on top of Parr Hill. Big enough to hold all of Beavertown—and then some. Son, "Junky Earl," interviewed in his eighties, remembered watching it go up when he was about ten or twelve years old.

Thought that it may have replaced an old log church house that stood on the other side of the road. Probably the United Brethren Church house which "Dragon John" mentioned in his sketch.

Official records of the Parr Hill church were destroyed long ago, so not much is known about its early beginnings. Named Parr Hill Fairview Church, it remained Beavertown's place of worship until the early nineteen hundreds. Next, William decided that the town needed a new school house.

Beaver children had been "schooled" in an old two-roomer located about half way up on Parr Hill (where "Johnny Boy" once lived). Many prominent people taught there: Grover Heddleston, Charles Brown, Clyde Paynter, Iva Keeler, Edna Fox, Glen Miller, Ann Harrington and Jessie Armstrong. (Eileen Thomas, *Washington Co. Ohio to 1980*)

Trading some of his own land for a choice spot down along State Route Seven, William planned and oversaw the building of the new school house. Turned out so well that he invited all children living in the surrounding area to attend—free of charge. At least twenty-five children showed up to be taught by a Mr. Nathaniel Kidd.

Then, in the late twenties, the state decided to transfer Beavertown children to Matamoras. What to do with this perfectly good building right there in their midst? With the old church house on the hill badly in need of repair, congregants decided to remodel the school house and meet there.

Abandoned, William's old church on the hill stood empty for years. In the late nineteen-hundreds, William's great grandson, David Beaver, decided to restore it and start holding services there once more.

With the help of Beavertown residents, the old place was cleaned up and restored to its original condition. Renamed Parr Hill Community Church, it now serves a thriving, growing congregation.

In the meantime, William's school house served Beavertown's religious needs well over the years. Various ministers came and went. Among them, Elmer Rogers, George Mendenhall and others. Last of all, Frank Conley.

Minister or no, services were always held with "Mutt" and Nellie Holdren—who lived next door—in charge. Sunday school classes every Sunday. Prayer meetings on Wednesday evenings. Consisted of singing (if no piano player present, a capella), praying and testifying.

Adults stood, and "testified" how God had helped them over the years. Reasserted their faith in the Lord, and promised to remain faithful for the rest of their lives.

Among those congregants, "Junky" Thompson's wife, Kate, who never missed a service. A great hulk of a woman, she stood well over six feet. Unable to buy regular shoes to fit her huge feet, she wore ankle top men's work shoes. Generally, laces untied.

Her long salt and pepper hair, she wore coiled atop her head. A generous amount of facial hair to match. Sounds fearsome, but totally harmless. Childlike in manner and thinking, she tramped up and down Beavertown's old gravel road, waving to those she happened to meet along the way.

Never intruded on neighbors. One exception. Always showed up to welcome every newborn in Beavertown.

Kate was not a native of Beavertown. Story goes that "Junky's" first wife "ran out on him," so he vowed to find himself "a wife no one else would want." Traveled up north and came back with Kate. Beavertown would not have been Beavertown without Kate.

Although not many adults attended regular church services, once a year, for the Christmas program, that church house would be filled to capacity. Beaming parents, grandparents and neighbors watched with pride as each child marched up front to say his "piece."

"Jiggs" Cochran's children, Gary and Donna were always the hit of the program. Just toddlers, they would walk hand in hand up to the pulpit platform and recite this old Christmas favorite:

Christmas is a-comin'
The goose is gittin' fat.
Please put a penny in the old man's hat.
If you ain't got a penny
A ha'penny'll do.
If ya ain't got a ha' penny
God bless you.

71

Program over, each child was given a "poke" (brown paper bag) of treats to take home.

In the 1960's, the congregation merged with the Methodist Church and was renamed the Beavertown United Methodist Church. Frank Conley became full time preacher and stayed for twenty-eight years.

Interviewed by *The Marietta Times* in September of 1988, he had nothing but good to say about Beavertown:

Beavertown is not as bad as the name carried down through history. I came in as a young minister. I was new. I've always had the freedom to worship there. It meant the world to me.

The town has a special quality that pulls it together when hard times fall on residents or visitors. Nobody every came to Beavertown hungry and left hungry.

When Conley retired, church services in William's school house came to an end. However, David Beaver's plans to reopen the old church on the hill were already underway. Now a whole new generation of Beavers (who know little or nothing about William Columbus) meets for worship there every Sunday.

Down in the valley, the old school house sits deserted, decaying and overgrown with vines, briars and brambles.

CHAPTER 15

$\mathcal{A}$s work on the dam came to an end, so did William's plans. In fact, many plans changed as young men returned home from the war in Europe. Short though it was, World War I would change the United States forever. Innovations like ready-made clothing, canned goods and modern appliances "freed women of much of household drudgery." Factories were humming. Henry Ford's new "Model T" now gave folks a freedom to travel to places never before accessible.

America went on a pleasure binge which would last for almost a decade—a period which would become known as the "Roaring Twenties."

Also returning, Prohibitionists, who had all but ceased their efforts to ban alcoholic drink during the war. One by one, states went dry. On January 17, 1920, their efforts paid off. The manufacture and sale of alcoholic beverages were banned completely.

News of the new source of booze spread like wildfire in a nation heretofore denied its number one sustenance. Although the name, Beavertown, could be found nowhere on maps of the time, (for that matter, not even today), few had little trouble finding it.

Did everyone in town end up in the whiskey business?

While Lyle Beaver did not, he knew everyone in town who did. Asked how many "Beavertowners" were not involved in the "moonshine" business, scratched his head and thought for a minute. "Only three. Richard Haught, 'Mutt' Holdren, and Bert McMasters."

Richard Haught lived about half way up the hill overlooking Beavertown. Only one connection with Beavers—the land on which he built his house had been purchased from none other than old "Dragon John."

"Mutt" Holdren lived "smack dab" in the heart of Beavertown, right next to the church where he served as Superintendent of Sunday School. "Never touched the stuff," but never complained—nor "snitched." Not even when a barrel of whiskey rolled off the hill and crashed into the back of his house.

As for "Burt" McMasters, he could "take it or leave it."

For that matter, "nobody ever turned anyone in." Except for a few angry housewives whose husbands drank too much. Then the law would come up from Marietta, locate the still and blow it up. Never came back to check.

Property lines were not always respected by "moonshiners." Myrtle Hutchison, who lived on the southern edge of Beavertown, went down under the river bank to pick corn beans one day. There sat a working still, right in the middle of the patch.

Myrtle had no quarrel with "moonshiners," per se. Indeed, some of her best friends lived up in Beavertown. But she was having no stills on her property.

Next day, she paid a visit to one of her Beaver friends, casually mentioning the still. "And if I go back tomorrow, and it's still there, I'm calling the law." Very next day, still was gone.

Spent mash barrels, by-products of stills, were something of a nuisance. Birds, squirrels, "coons," chickens—all loved that mash. Nothing funnier than a crazy drunken chicken. Even cows, given the chance would eat themselves into a drunken bundle of bones, almost impossible to move.

Eunice Beaver's old red cow could smell a mash barrel a mile away. If she did not come home by milking time, someone had to go looking for her. Nine chances out of ten, she had found a mash barrel, eaten her fill and was too drunk to even get up.

Took more than one to get her up and off the hill. Then hold her up for milking. After all that, her milk had to be thrown away or fed to the pigs. No longer fit for human consumption. Finally, fed up with her shenanigans, Eunice took her down to Marietta and sold her.

Living anywhere near Beavertown could be entertaining—or irritating—depending on one's point of view. For those living north of Beavertown, a bit of both. Every spring, the Ohio River flooded sections of Route Seven, halting all traffic for a few days.

Some of Beavertown's loyal patrons simply could not stand being cut off from their main source of refreshment. Took to the hills above the river on foot. Actually, just a pleasant stroll—that is—on the way down. Coming back, very hazardous indeed.

Frank Cochran, who lived up on the hill overlooking Route Seven just south of Matamoras, dreaded those spring floods. Almost without fail, some "loaded" pedestrian making his way back from Beavertown would end up down in the muddy, chilly flood waters below.

Daughter Joan said, "We lost count of how many 'drunks' Dad had to rescue over the years. After fishing them out, had to drag them up over the hill, strip off their wet clothes and wrap them in an old Indian blanket."

"Mom took the sodden clothes and hung them over a chair in front of the fireplace to dry, then put on the coffee pot. Managed to get a couple cups of strong coffee into the trembling fellows before they nodded off."

In a couple hours or so, they would "come to." With a little help, struggle into their clothes which had dried "stiff as a board." Still shaking like a leaf and apologizing profusely, off they would shuffle toward their intended destination.

That was not the Cochran's only contact with Beavertown's "moonshine" business. The hills up behind the house fairly bristled with stills. Cochran children were forbidden to go beyond a certain point. Not because of any animosity between Cochrans and "moonshiners." Mr. Cochran and still operators were on quite friendly terms.

Daughter Joan said, "Sometimes Dad would take the boys—never the girls—on a hike up through 'forbidden territory.' The boys generally came back with their pockets jingling with what I assumed to be 'hush' money."

At any one time during Prohibition, it was impossible to pass through Beavertown's hills without coming on a still. Needless to say, trails through those woods were well worn. One old codger traversed those hills almost daily. Always carried an empty Prince Albert tobacco can in one shirt pocket. Just in case.

With so many different operations, a bit of rivalry developed among "moonshiners." (Illustrated by this little tale courtesy of "Cotton.")

One operator, particularly skilled in the art of making whiskey guarded his operation jealously. Allowed no one near his property, nor gave anyone as much as a "sniff" of his wares.

Unfortunately, the law caught up with him one day. Hauled him off to Marietta where he was sentenced to six months in jail, which set off a regular "treasure hunt" for his "stash."

Although Beavers were not given to much drinking, some of the younger bunch could not stand it. Were just dying to get a taste of that stuff.

After searching the hills in vain, they decided to tackle the wife. Maybe she would at least give them a clue.

"Nothing doing." However, they finally wore her down. She consented to give them "one clue, but that was it." Only three words. "A dry place. That's it, and don't come back anymore."

"Cotton" laughed. "We all knew when they found it."

Not all "moonshiners" were so secretive. Some, like George Remus, made little effort to hide their prosperity. In fact, made an open show of their newly found wealth.

Beavertown had its own version of George Remus. Always drove latest model cars and threw money around like confetti.

Periodically, held square dances in the big old barn in the center of town. Open to the public, attracted dancers from all over the valley. Two ten-gallon buckets of whiskey—equipped with long handled dippers—were set up at each end of the dance floor. Refilled as needed all night long.

Halfway through the dance, intermission. Freezers of homemade ice cream and various kinds of cakes were brought out. Again, free of charge. Reinforced, dancers returned to their dancing into the wee hours of the morning.

Although Matamoras residents tended to "look down their noses" at Beavertown, many could be found among those dancers. Lyle said, "They needn't have felt so superior. Whiskey money was about all that kept Matamoras afloat during the depression."

Because of its nearness to Beavertown, Matamoras was something of a party town for "Roaring Twentiers" far and near. Tales about those times were many and varied, but only this one (provided by local historian Diana McMahan), perhaps because of its very nature, survives:

One prominent family, entertaining out of town guests for the weekend, had partied well into the night. Next morning, they came straggling down—one by one—for breakfast. Time passed and one guest had yet to make an appearance.

"Guess the poor old guy couldn't take it," laughed one of the guests. "Somebody better go up and check on him. He may be dead."

The ladies had a better idea. "Let's go out and pick some flowers for him. Out they went, picked a nice bouquet, and headed up the stairs, giggling all the way.

About to lay the flowers on his chest, they drew back in horror. The old guy really was dead. (True story.)

Although most Matamoras folks simply bought their whiskey down in Beavertown, a few attempted to make their own. Don Mark Holdren remembered one of his uncles who decided to go that route.

"He set up a still out in the woods, sat down to watch and promptly fell asleep. The thing blew up and 'dang near' killed him."

A very small group of individuals living about a mile or so south of Beavertown, were more successful. No connection to Beavertown at all.

Catering to some of Marietta's elite (who would not have been "caught dead" buying their supply of whiskey in Beavertown), they survived the hard times very well. Survived with barely a hint of what had been going on there for thirteen years.

How did they manage that? For one thing, stills were located far from their own property. Some even across the river on the West Virginia shore. Premises around their houses, clean as a whistle. Not a single sign of anything untoward.

Up in Beavertown, wives were an essential part of the whiskey business. Wives down there would not have "touched a still with a ten-foot pole." Any reference to whiskey within the confines of the home, strictly forbidden.

Business transactions, conducted Sunday afternoons after church. Customers would drive up from Marietta in their big, shiny black cars. Park in shady secluded spots and spend an hour or so just visiting. At some point during their stay, merchandise would be surreptitiously slipped into their cars.

Of course, those living in the area knew exactly what was going on. Especially with children boarding the school bus dressed only in the finest the Montgomery Ward catalog had to offer. Wives sported beauty shop hairdos and groceries delivered right to the door. Other tell-tale signs that there was money somewhere.

No matter, "moonshine" buyers were looking for just one thing. That BEAVERTOWN UNINCORPORATED sign, which marked the beginning of three solid miles of "moonshine" houses.

CHAPTER 16

$\mathcal{F}$irst group of houses inside the Beavertown sign, was inhabited not by Beavers, but by Cochrans. No information as to when they settled there. No connection to Beavers. (Except for two marriages. Rob Cochran to Mildred Beaver and Clarence "Slopy" Cochran to Icy Beaver.) But "moonshine" was definitely available there.

Carl and Stella Cochran lived in the big house on the hill. Their children—Ray, Helen and Beryl—lived in smaller houses built around them.

Ray and his wife, Hazel, first built their house just across the highway from Ray's parents. Constant flooding of the Ohio River finally forced them to move the entire house over to the bank on the right side of the "home place." Their five children—William, Edward, Louella, Darrell and Dean grew up there.

Helen married "Ike" Miracle, or Merckle. They had two daughters, Betty and Lucille. Sometime after the girls married, the whole family moved to Florida and spent the rest of their lives there.

Beryl married Chester Heddleston. Their house sat on the upper side of Old Beavertown Road. Out of all those houses, the only one still standing. In a thicket of ghostly gray trees. Three children grew up there. John, Ruby (Allen) and Robert. All deceased.

A bit to the right, down on the very edge of the highway, stands a big two story house. During Prohibition, home to Clarence "Slopy"

Cochran and his wife Icy Beaver Cochran. (Now occupied by Douglas and Kathy Cochran—unrelated.)

Icy and "Slopy" Cochran had four children. Doris, Vernon ("Jiggs"), Charles ("Chuck") and Jack.

To the right of "Slopy," stood a small house belonging to his brother "Rob." Just above "Rob," on Old Beavertown Road, stood the house of Carl Cochran (father of "Rob," "Slopy" and Ralph "Drakey"). Ralph and his wife, Alma, lived right across Old Beavertown Road from the parents.

Were the Cochrans involved in the "moonshine" business? Indeed. "Slopy," along with "Riddle" Beaver and Veryl "Cotton" Beaver (Icy's nephew) were among the very first to try their hand at making whiskey. And never stopped until the bitter end.

In the 1980's, when research for this history began, both "Slopy" and "Riddle" were in their graves, but "Cotton" was still very much "alive and kicking." Questioned about his "moonshine" adventures, was absolutely delighted to talk about those days. Here, a small sample:

I loved making that stuff. We first set up shop about a mile north of Beavertown, down along the Ohio River shore, just below Jim and Becky Flowers' house. Jim and Becky never would have turned us in, so we always operated in full view of the old couple.

In appreciation, always filled up the quart Mason jar which Becky would leave out on the stoop now and then.

Since most of their customers were over in West Virginia, that location suited us perfectly. Business was conducted at night. We would wait for a signal (lantern or flashlight), load the whiskey into a skiff and paddle silently across the river and back.

Gangsters from Youngstown, Ohio, were some of our best customers. For some reason known only to them, they preferred to take delivery on the West Virginia side of the river.

Business finally "got so good" that we had to find a bigger place. Choosing a secluded hollow all the way down at the southern end of Beavertown—across from what would later become Heiney's Gulf Station—we set up nine stills in a "V" shaped formation up the hollow.

Everything went smoothly until the day one of our stills caught fire, threatening to engulf the surrounding woods. Ordinarily, we could have snuffed it out without much trouble, but there had been scarcely any rain that summer. Everything was tinder dry. Fortunately, we were able to extinguish the flames before anyone came to investigate.

After all those years, did he still remember how to make whiskey? Better believe it.

COTTON'S INSTRUCTIONS

(With a few extra comments thrown in here and there.)

Making whiskey is not very complicated. All you need is a copper boiler, copper coils and a fifty gallon barrel. The coil's the main thing. Old "Bub" Beaver made one out of his wife's empty snuff cans. State men who discovered it could not bring themselves to destroy it. Carried it off intact and had it written up in the paper.

First, you take 30–35 pounds of rye. In the beginning, we used corn, also dried peaches. Made wonderful whiskey. Add about 75 pounds of sugar and five cakes of yeast. Later, we were able to get real brewer's yeast.

At first, we had to test it by taste, then used a rudimentary alcohol tester. Finally, we got hold of a real government tester which told temperature and strength. Periodically, our local doctor would test it and pronounced it "purer than store bought."

We learned to set barrels into the ground about three feet—which would hasten the process as much as three days. Earth formations can still be found in the woods around Beavertown, marking places where barrels had been partly buried.

We never had to go looking for buyers. Once a week, a truck came from Charleston, West Virginia, pulled into my garage and loaded up fifty to seventy-five gallons. In the beginning, we were getting twenty dollars a gallon. Then it got down to only two dollars. However, some customers like Fred Stover "shelled out" fifty dollars for five gallons to the very end. Finally, prices got so low that you could buy a pint for just fifty cents.

Former Matamoras resident, George Henning (interviewed by *The Times* on August 11, 2012), said much the same thing:

It was a big deal around Beavertown (Ohio). During the great depression, they had their stills away from the houses up in the woods. There was a lot of "moonshine" made and sold—you could buy a pint of "moonshine" for fifty cents.

While falling prices played a big part in the demise of the "moonshine" market, there were also other forces at work. Law enforcement was slowly but surely closing in.

"Almost breathing down our necks." Local authorities not so much, but state men with no connections to Beavertown. We got to know a lot of them by name—Old Frew, Jessie Love and some others." ("Cotton")

Actually, establishment of the WPA did as much or more to bring down the "moonshine" trade than anything else. Dubbed "We Piddle Around" by locals, it provided gainful employment for Beavers and many, many others.

"And you know," grinned "Cotton," having money in your pocket puts a whole new 'shine' on things."

[A few of those old WPA projects still stand. Not long ago, the bridge leading out of Matamoras into the country was replaced. At its entrance, pressed right into the concrete in big bold letters — "Project of the WPA."]

Growing up in a house where alcoholic beverages were strictly forbidden had precious little effect on nine-year-old "Cotton." Free to wander — as most Beaver children were — he often ended up at Uncle "Slopy's" place. When "Slopy" and "Riddle" set up their first still, "Cotton" joined them and stayed to the end.

For the most part, "moonshiners" had little to fear from law enforcement. Lyle said that all kinds of arrangements between Beavertown and the law took care of that. Here is how it all went down:

There were periodic meetings between the law and "moonshiners." State officials had to notify the sheriff in Marietta when they were coming into his territory. The sheriff would then get word to Beavers that the "Bulls" were on the way. He might even go along and show them the way, avoiding places where stills might be located.

Sheriffs were under few restraints then, conducting business much as they saw fit. I knew a sheriff who was called to the home of an elderly couple living back of Matamoras. On the first of every month, their two grown sons would wait for the mail and steal their parents' old age pension checks. Then off they would go into town and spend it all on drinking and carousing until the money was gone. Go back home and laze around, waiting for the next check to come.

On his way to the farm, the sheriff stopped and cut off a long willow switch. Then on to the farm where he found the two lounging around while their parents toiled away out in the garden. "Whaled the daylights" out of them; made them promise to never do it again or he would be back. That was the end of their "shenanigans."

Without Lyle, this history never would have been written. He was the one and only source of information about "Dragon John." (From Lyle, in the Beaver family and friends picture shown earlier, he is the dark haired little boy standing just behind the little girl sitting next to "Dragon John."

Even at that tender age, he was already cutting hair, practicing on anyone who would sit still for him. Following, his version of how he began barbering—as told to Roger Kalter in 1988:

I had a barber shop when I was 12 years old cutting kid's hair. I cut for 10 cents. If they didn't have a dime, I didn't charge them. I learned on "Cooney" Danver. He never had any money so I cut his hair for free.

"Got pretty good at it, but was afraid to tackle shaving by myself. Closed my shop and headed for Matamoras—which at that time had seven full-time barber shops."

Approached barber Bill Gautschi and made him this proposition: "I would work for him for a year—without pay—if he would teach me to shave. We shook on it, and I stayed my year."

At year's end, he crossed the river to Sistersville, West Virginia, and opened his own shop. "Was doing quite well," when the Yeast Foam Company offered him a job representing the company on the road. For a lot more than he could ever make barbering. (Yeast Foam was very busy during Prohibition. Made "oodles" of money selling yeast to "bootleggers.")

Might have stayed on with Yeast Foam, but Jewel Tea Company lured him away with more money. He spent six more years on the road. During that period, he met and married a Matamoras girl, Ruth Moyer. Together they decided that it was time to come home.

Finding a spot in a big building up in Fly, Ohio—which also housed a meat shop and a pool hall—Lyle again opened a barber shop. One year later, traded shops with Tommy Oaf down in Matamoras and cut hair there for nine years.

"Moonshining" was in full swing by then; both Beavertown and Matamoras—busy places. Beavertown, because of its "moonshine" business. Matamoras, because of the "moonshine" money being spent there.

Running a barber shop kept Lyle a little too busy to actually go into the "moonshine" business for himself. However, he and fellow barber, Bruce English, decided that they could make a lot more money by establishing a "whiskey route" around through the back country.

At that time, whiskey was sold in quart and gallon Mason jars— twenty dollars per quart. They purchased fifteen quarts—fourteen for selling and one for sampling. (However, failed to take into account the time-honored custom of sealing every bargain by sharing a drink.)

By the time they got to Graysville, Ohio, they had run out of whiskey and were in no condition to drive. End of whiskey route.

Although barbering kept Lyle busy, he still found time to visit Beavertown regularly. After all, most of his relatives still lived there. Every day, promptly at noon, he would signal Mr. Little, owner of the shoe repair shop across the street. They would close up and drive the six miles down to "Slopy" Cochran's cellar for a cold beer. "Slopy" was well-known for superb beer—as well as whiskey.

[A little sidenote here about his nickname. When asked why he only used one "p" in his name, replied, "I only use one 'p' in 'Slopy' because two 'p's' is too sloppy."]

He was also known for miles around as a very skilled carpenter. When Doug and Kathy Cochran, (not related) bought "Slopy's" house in 1971, they discovered a picture of a still in an old Buffet in his work-shop. In their words:

We found this picture in an old Buffet in Clarence ("Slopy") Cochran's workshop at his residence we bought in 1971. "Slopy" was still living at the time. The still was set up behind our house on the hill. Our house was full of "moonshiner" history—cubby holes every where to hide the evidence. The attic you could walk the entire length which held "moonshine." This still was identified by "Slopy" as one of his first stills. His son, Vernon ("Jiggs") Cochran told us many stories of this.

One of Beavertown's first stills in actual operation during Prohibition. Barely discernable is the "moonshine" flowing through the copper pipe into the bucket at the lower right of the barrel.

When Prohibition ended, Lyle and Ruth moved back to Canton, Ohio, where he opened up another barber shop. Continued barbering until he left for the army on June 29, 1943.

After the war, he and Ruth bought a big house in the center of Matamoras, right next to the one red light in town. Ruth opened a frozen custard shop on one side of the house—Lyle, a barber shop on the other.

After Ruth passed away, he remained in that house on the corner. Continued barbering, but at a much slower pace. He died suddenly of a heart attack in 1989. He was eighty-two years old. Had he lived longer, this history might have been a lot longer.

Fortunately, he was not the only source of material for this writing. Eunice Beaver outlived him by almost twenty years. She knew the "moonshine" business inside and out and then some.

CHAPTER 17

"$\mathcal{D}$oc" and Eunice Beaver were actually late comers to the business. Reason? Eunice was "dead set agin' it." On the other hand, "Doc" was just "itchin' to get in." Behind Eunice's back—with the help of "Griz" Beaver, he set up a barrel of mash out in the barn. ("Doc" had contracted measles when he was three, resulting in damage to his eyes. So he could not see to do it by himself.)

One day Eunice heard the old hens cackling out in the barn and went to investigate. Found the barrel and threatened to upset it.

"They talked me out of it, promising to move it when it was ready to run. Of course, they'd have to use my kitchen for that. Reluctantly I agreed. Just this one time."

Time for "running" came all too soon. Eunice put the kids to bed early. Waited for "Griz" and another fellow to come, then went to bed herself.

Lying there listening to their hurried movements and worried whispering, she could not resist. Getting out of bed, she dressed quickly and slipped out the back door. Picking up an old tomato stake, she made her way silently around to the front.

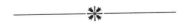

I took that stake and rapped on the door twice. (Just like law men did with the barrels of their guns.) Dead silence. I knocked again, and they took off like scared rabbits. Out of the kitchen, through the pantry and out onto the little back porch covered with chicken wire to keep out the "varmints." They went right through, chicken wire and all.

Had anyone told Eunice that she would someday end up in the "moonshine" business—in a place called Beavertown—she would not have believed it.

Born in 1892—somewhere between Bloomfield and Archers Fork, (actually Tadpole Run) Eunice knew little about the outside world. But she surely hoped to.

As luck would have it, one of her father's sisters, from East Liverpool, Ohio, came for a visit. All "dolled up" in the latest fashions, she regaled the family with tales of street cars, electric lights and all the amenities of city living. From that time on, getting up to East Liverpool was her main goal.

About the only way to make money in that era lay in big cities like Wellsburg, West Virginia. On the Ohio side of the river, East Liverpool and Steubenville. Periodically, Mr. Pritchard would leave home and search for work in one of those places.

Finally, tiring of being away from home so much, he decided to "pull up stakes" and move the whole family to his next work site. In the meantime, Mrs. Pritchard would sell everything—except a few necessities and get ready to make the move. He would "get word" to them when he was established well enough to send for them.

All excited, they followed his instructions, preparing to leave on a moment's notice. That "word" was a long time coming. For good reason. Mr. Pritchard had fallen off the roof where he was working and hurt his back. Still recuperating in the Steubenville hospital.

What a pickle! There they were, with only the clothes on their backs and little else. Only one place to go. Grandma's house over on Archers Fork. Crest fallen, they set out—on foot, Mom and kids, over the long dusty trek to Archers Fork.

Time passed and still no word from Dad. Leaves on the trees turned from green to yellow and gold. Eunice could wait no longer. Talked her mother into letting her go to Wellsburg to check on her father. A bit past sixteen now, she was old enough to take care of herself. Besides, they did have relatives in Steubenville—somewhere.

With Mom's reluctant permission, Eunice hitched a ride into Matamoras. Arrived just in time to catch the ferry over to Friendly, West Virginia. Boarded the train heading north to Wellsburg and arrived there safely without incident.

After making inquiries, Eunice learned that her relatives lived some nine miles out in the country. Undaunted, set out on foot and managed to find them without much trouble.

But I sure didn't like it there. Left after two weeks. Walked all the way back to Wellsburg. Made it just about dark and managed to find her father's boarding house.

The lady who ran the place was all in a "dither." Her help had just sent word that she was ill and unable to come to work. And right there at supper time. I stepped in and took over. The landlady was so relieved and impressed that she would have hired me on the spot. But I had other plans.

Did not have to stay there long. Mr. Pritchard was suddenly given some time off and decided to visit one of his sisters up in East Liverpool. Eunice could come along if she wanted, but she had to come right back with him. To make sure, made her pack her clothes in her suitcase, then hid it.

With the help of her sympathetic landlady, Eunice found the suitcase. Took out two of everything, put them on, one over the other. Looking a bit pudgy, she boarded the train and never looked back.

Arriving safely in East Liverpool, they soon found Mr. Pritchard's sister's house and settled in. Actually, Eunice did. Mr. Pritchard soon headed off to see if he could find some of his "old drinking cronies."

Writing down directions to another aunt's house on the other side of the city, Eunice picked up her spare belongings and set out.

In her long skirts, hair twisted into a knot atop her head, she clopped along, ignoring the stares and titters of those she encountered along the way.

First thing she did on arriving at her aunt's house was borrow a pair of scissors. Bobbed her hair and shortened her long skirts. "Did a pretty good job, too—even if I do say so myself."

Eunice could not have arrived in East Liverpool at a better time. The pottery industry was at its peak and hiring lots of women. She had little trouble finding work. Was soon earning enough to cover her "board and keep" and then some.

Busy though she was, before long, began to miss her family. Surely Dad had forgiven her for running off by now. Had to chance it, anyway. So she packed her suitcase once more and boarded the train for home.

Arrived home, only to find that nothing had changed. Not only had Mr. Pritchard not forgiven her, he forbade her to ever leave home again. Once again, confiscated her suitcase containing all her clothes and hid it. Her mother was watching and saw where he hid it. Retrieved it in the middle of the night and "snuk" it over to Grandma's.

"I left in the middle of the night, picked up my suitcase from Grandma's house, and made my way to Matamoras. Took the ferry back across the river to Friendly, and boarded the next train for East Liverpool.

So—if she couldn't go back home, the family would just have to come up to East Liverpool. She knew just how to do that. Find a job in East Liverpool for Mr. Prichard. He'd never pass up a chance to make some money.

Orchards would be hiring pickers soon, and she began making her rounds. Found him a job picking apples and "sent word" for him to come. He was on the very next train to East Liverpool. That was the easy part. Bringing up the rest of the family, that would take some doing.

For one thing, they had no clothes fit for traveling. Guessing at sizes, she began shopping—one or two articles of clothing out of every paycheck. By the end of summer she had assembled an outfit for each sibling. Packed them all into a big suitcase, and boarded the train for Friendly once more.

Most of the clothing fit fairly well. Except one brother's jacket was way too big. To correct that, she just had one brother walk closely behind him, "cinching in" the back. From the front, looked a perfect fit.

Thus outfitted, the family headed for Matamoras. Arrived too late to catch the train heading north, so had to stay the night there. Next morning, herded them all onto the ferry. Back across the river, and onto the train. Good-bye Tadpole Run forever.

Mission accomplished, Eunice settled down to work in the pottery and enjoy everything which city-life had to offer. Three years passed without incident. Then fate intervened. In the form of this handsome apple picker from Beavertown, Ohio—Raymond Beaver.

After a whirlwind courtship, they were married on July 17, 1915. He brought her home to Beavertown—where she would spend the rest of her life.

CHAPTER 18

"**D**oc's" father gave them a lot right next door, where they built their first house.

RAYMOND "DOC" AND EUNICE BEAVER

THEIR FIRST HOUSE
Sadly, that house burned to the ground and they had to rebuild.

When Eunice arrived in Beavertown, the place was buzzing with activity. Construction on Dam Sixteen was going full blast, with every able-bodied Beaver employed—even men from far away as New York.

Because of his poor eyesight, "Doc" could not work directly on the dam, but got a job ferrying workers back and forth across the river. Granddaughter Eileen Thomas said, "while he could not see to do close work, there was nothing wrong with his thinking. He was a 'whiz' at math." Often helped her with homework, especially those "horrible reading problems." She would read a problem to him. He would give her the answer, then make her work it out.

Had he been able to see, "Doc" could have written a book about his earlier life. Made up for that by regaling folks with tales about his many and varied experiences. One night, buoyed up by several glasses of hard cider, kept the Hutchison family on the edges of their seats listening well past midnight.

"Dragon John" had been in his grave up in Parr Hill Cemetery two years when "Doc" returned home for good with Eunice. By that time, "Doc's" youngest brother, Harman, was living in John's house. Other members of the family settled in homes strung out along the hillside.

Elmer, who is said to have introduced Beavers to the art of "moonshine" making, lived just across Parr Hill Road from William Columbus. He died and his widow inherited his house.

Later, a Martin family lived in that house for some time. Others unknown. Finally, it was just torn down. That space remained empty for years. Then one of Elmer's descendants, Bill Beaver, came to Beavertown and built a house on the empty lot.

Everything went fine until wife Ann got sick. She died and Bill did not stay long after that. Ended up selling it to some folks from out of town. Left Beavertown, never to return.

Across Parr Hill Road from Elmer's house, stood a big two-story house built and occupied by "Doc's" father, William Columbus. (After William and his wife died, occupied by daughters Daisy Sole and Sylvia Abbot.) A mobile home now sits on that location.

Eunice said, "When I arrived there were no homes close to us." Some distance to the south, sat one caught by "Lyle and others during a flood." "We pulled it in and tied it to the bank near a log house where old Mr. McCall lived. When time came to move it, Mr. McCall made us pay for crossing his property." (Lyle)

[Several different families lived in that house over the years—including the writer and her family. Louis and Alma Thomas were the last. Lonnie Beaver ("Cotton's" son) finally bought it and tore it down.]

Lew and Jim Beaver, contractors from "up north," (Beavers from another branch of the Beaver family tree.) built the two houses next in line. Jim built the first one. He and his first wife are said to have lived there until their divorce. Later "Cotton" and Eloise Beaver moved in and raised their four children there—William, Patty, Charlotte and Lonnie.

Bachelor Lew dated both of William Columbus' daughters—Sylvia and Ollie, but could not seem to choose between the two. However, circumstances forced the issue and William arranged a "shotgun" (a real shotgun) wedding. Hauled Lew and Ollie off to the preacher, stood by for the ceremony and sent them packing.

The newlyweds began married life on a houseboat anchored on the shore at Sistersville, West Virginia. Later, moved "up north" and remained there for the rest of their lives. (Interesting little note here—when Ollie died, Lew came back, married Sylvia and took her back "up north" with him.)

Jim Beaver remarried. A local girl, Laura Wines. Later, suffered a stroke. Unable to get around, he and Laura, moved to a small house on Third Street up in Matamoras. Spent the rest of his life sitting in a window facing the street, watching the rest of the world go by.

That would have been in the early forties, for the writer used to pass that house on the way to school. Jim was always there, sitting in that window, reading or just watching folks come and go.

The house which Jim had built in Beavertown became home to newlyweds, Earl and Blanch Beaver. Not long after, it caught fire and burned to the ground. "Griz," who had recently built a house just across the road, took them in. Later, Earl moved out, leaving just "Griz" and Blanche. After "Griz" died, Blanche remained there until her death. That house, at this time, remains in reasonably good condition.

To the south next to "Griz," a huge tract of land belonging to the McCall family. They lived in a log house built down by the riverside (where Route Seven now runs).

Four daughters grew up there—Nettie, Molly, Nellie and Mima. All except Mima ended up marrying and building houses on that property.

Nellie married "Mutt" Holdren—one son, Gene (Klel). Nettie also married a Holdren—her son, Claude, drowned while working on the wickets over on the dam.

Mima married Jack Haught. They lived in a house right next to "Doc" and Eunice. Once belonged to Fred Beaver. (Lyle said that for some reason, Fred sold that house and built another one on the river side of the Beavertown Road.) Jack and "Mime" raised three children there—Gladys Cole, Evelyn Hutchison and Herman.

The McCall's property ended at a little stream separating the northern and southern halves of Beavertown. First house on the other side of that stream occupied by Clem Wilson. At the beginning of "moonshine" days, "Snappin' Charlie" bought it, raised his family and ran his "moonshine" business from there. With the end of Prohibition, sold it and bought the huge tract of land just south of Beavertown. Built his famous "beer joint" there and ran it until his death.

Over the years, that house was home to a number of families. In the late forties or early fifties, Charlie's son, "Raybo," bought it. He and Dorthy moved back into the house where "Raybo" grew up.

When "Raybo" died, Dorthy continued living there until her sight failed. No longer able to live alone, she moved to The Arbors nursing home in Marietta, Ohio. Later to a nursing home near her daughter, Shelda Cloud, in Bellview, Ohio, where she passed away. (Dorthy was a major contributor to this history.)

After Dorthy's death, her house stood empty for a time. Folks from out of town, the Rugurios, bought it. Remodeled and landscaped to within an inch of its life, it now bears little resemblance to the old house. But still stands solid as a rock.

Next house to the south belonged to Jim Wines, who later sold it to Vernon "Jiggs" Cochran. "Jiggs" raised his family there. That house marks the boundary between Beavers and Cochrans. Empty at this writing.

Southern end, no Beavers at all, only Cochrans. No clue as to when the first Cochrans arrived in the area. Berry's book of early settlers lists just one—Zacheriah Cochran. In 1837, acquired several acres of land in what is now called Grandview. No information as to when other Cochrans arrived in the area.

So Eunice did not know much about the Cochrans. Between building their house and starting a family, she had little time to think about who or what lay beyond the Wilson house. Raising five children kept her, like most women of the time, busy from sun up to sundown. From eldest to youngest:

Mildred (Middy) Cochran Smith
Vernon (Johnny Boy)
Margaret (Jiggs) Berga
Raymond (Bugs)
Dean

Mildred first married Rob Cochran, (One of only two Beaver/Cochran marriages.) When Rob died, married Joe Smith. No children. Died at Heartland of Marietta nursing home at ripe of old age of one hundred three.

Margaret married Charles "Chuck" Berga during Prohibition times. "Chuck" was a big burly guy who fit right into the "moonshine" business. Is said to have escaped capture many times by simply tossing his pursuers into a mash barrel. Did not always help. According to daughter Peggy Taylor, one time he came limping home with a bullet in his leg.

"Chuck" and Margaret had four children—Eileen Thomas (deceased), James (deceased), Peggy Taylor (deceased) and Linda Rinard.

Doc and Eunice's second child, John (Johnny Boy) married Amy June Heddleson. Six children—Dick, Kenny, Mary, Judy, Fred and John.

"Johnny Boy" grew up during Prohibition, running afoul of the law on various occasions. Most memorable, his encounter with Matamoras town marshal, John Boles.

Driving home from Matamoras one day, he was pulled over by Boles. Suspecting that "Johnny" might be carrying a load of "moonshine," Boles ordered him out of the car, then proceeded to search it.

Made the mistake of leaving his patrol car running. "Johnny" ran back, jumped into the patrol car and took off down Route Seven. Boles climbed into "Johnny's" car and gave chase. Down Route Seven they went—all the way to Beavertown and up over Parr Hill Road. Boles right on "Johnny's" tail.

At the top of the hill, "Johnny" crashed the patrol car and took off up into the woods. Nothing the marshal could do except "bum a ride" back to town. Johnny stayed hidden up in the woods for some time.

Friends tried to talk him into giving himself up, but he refused. When Boles finally gave up looking for him, he resurfaced. Lyle said, "But nothing ever came of it. You know, they had 'connections' in Marietta."

Raymond "Bugs" Beaver was born too late to be part of "moonshine" days. He married and built a house down on Route Seven, just south of his parents' house. His wife died at a very young age. Three children. Debbie, Toni and Mike.

Dean married, divorced. When Mildred's husband (Joe) died, he moved in and took care of her until health issues forced her into Heartland of Marietta where she died.

In the aftermath of World War I, high tariffs and crop surpluses, along with a lack of work, set farmers like the Beavers back on their heels.

Eunice said it was the worst time ever. "Money was as scarce as hen's teeth." From that time on, there was no stopping the flow of "moonshine" from the little town. However, Eunice wanted no part of it.

Perhaps because of her father's drinking habits, she refused to have anything to do with it. She hadn't counted on "Doc" and "Griz," who were bent of starting their own whiskey business.

Finally, she could resist no longer. She and "Doc" ended up running what she called, "the premier whiskey operation of the valley. And we were the only ones never once hauled into court." Here are some ways in which they used to make and distribute most of their product:

We soon learned that making whiskey from scratch had its drawbacks. For one thing, more chance of getting caught. So we ended up purchasing "green" whiskey from others and aging it ourselves. Never, never sold "green" whiskey.

Aging is the secret of making good whiskey. We aged it in fifty–two gallon barrels—charred on the inside—purchased from a supplier up in northern Ohio. Three months was the preferred time, but the longer, the better.

I had a special way which produced some of the very best. I kept a keg full in our bedroom right next to a small gas heater. Every time I passed by, would stop and shake it up a little—really made it good. (Eunice)

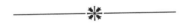

They had two hard and fast rules—sold only by five-gallon kegs—or jugs. And never from their house. However, word of their "business" somehow reached all the way to Canton, Ohio. (Canton was the main supplier of containers for "bootleggers" during Prohibition.)

One day a truck which they had never seen before pulled up to their garage. Driver got out, opened the doors and drove in. Without a word, unloaded dozens of jugs, backed out, closed the doors, climbed back into his truck and drove off.

"We hadn't ordered them. Never did know who sent them. Of course, we had many friends in high places."

If they never sold from their house, how did they manage to serve so many customers? In various and sundry ways. A keg of whiskey—ordered by an elder of the Baptist Church in Reno, Ohio, was delivered in this manner:

Most churches then had no inside plumbing, so each was equipped with an outside "restroom." Reno's was located right on the edge of Route Seven. Although intended for parishioners only, it was used regularly by folks traveling up and down the highway. (No rest stops then.)

Anyone stopping there aroused no suspicions at all, so delivery was accomplished with no suspicion or interference.

We would pull up to the toilet as close as possible. One of us would get out, go in and hold the door open enough to roll a keg of whiskey inside.

We would stay a bit—maybe even use the facility. Come out, close the door and continue on our way.

Although much of Beavertown whiskey was sold locally, some ended up in far-away places. One enterprising "moonshiner" took a truck load all the way to New York City. Arrived at the designated place of delivery without any trouble, only to find the place crawling with cops. All engaged in smashing everything to "smithereens."

Nothing like that would ever happen in Beavertown. There was the occasional dynamiting of a still which someone had reported. Hardly made a dent in the hundreds operating everywhere. Down under the river bank, under porches, in the kitchens—just name it.

"Doc" and Eunice were the exception. They rarely operated a still at all. Mostly bought "green" whiskey from smaller outfits, then aged it themselves. Greatly reduced their chances of getting caught.

Their "ace in the hole" was none other than the sheriff of Washington County. Once a month he drove up from Marietta to collect one five gallon keg of whiskey. According to Eunice, this is how it went:

We knew his car. He would drive up alone, "just for a friendly, visit." Driving into our garage, he'd come out, shut the doors and head up to the house.

Would stay and chat for a while. "Doc" already had his keg ready, and would slip down and put it in his car while it was in the garage. That was the routine.

Unlike "Doc" and Eunice, many Beavers sold to almost anyone who knocked on their doors. For instance: While a student at Harvard, Dr. Richard Hamilton of St. Marys, West Virginia, brought one of his class mates home for a visit.

Intending to show him places of interest in the valley, was quite taken aback when the one place his friend wanted to go was Beavertown.

Dr. Hamilton dutifully drove him up Route Seven to Beavertown. Waited in the car while his friend climbed some steps to a big white house on the hill. (Almost all Beaver houses sat upon a hill.) Came back carrying a brown paper bag containing bottles of Beavertown whiskey.

Word of Beavertown whiskey spread to the rest of the country in many ways. On a trip down through the valley, a salesman from Akron, Ohio, was given a taste of that whiskey. Drove straight home, tore the back seat out of his car and built in a secret compartment. Made more money selling Beavertown whiskey than he ever made with his regular goods.

For an enterprising bellhop down at Marietta's Lafayette Hotel, Beavertown whiskey paid off big time. His story is said to have been printed on the backs of the hotel's place mats at one time. A copy of that story follows—exactly as it appeared on that mat. (From the files of Eileen Thomas.)

THE CASE OF THE BOOTLEGGING BELLHOP

General suspicions became concrete during the flood in the early thirties. How could a bellhop afford a shiny new Ford Coupe while attending the Marietta Commercial College? Why was this generally quiet, lanky bellhop so liked by the regular guests? Quite a few "Ah-Hah's" were heard around the Lafayette Hotel at that point during Prohibition.

The lower level of the hotel was taking on water. Lo and behold what would come floating up the main lobby steps but a half dozen pint bottles of what would later be determined to be "moonshine."

As the story is told, "Skinny," the enterprising bellhop, was making trips to the Beavertown, Ohio area where he would purchase a gallon of illegal liquor for five dollars. In a remote cubby under the main lobby stairs he would re-bottle the "shine" and sell it for two-fifty a pint. The elevator at that time required an operator and often the operator was "Skinny." On the trip down for dinner a guest would slip "Skinny" their room key and the appropriate tip. "Skinny" would leave the booze in the guest's room, and on the return trip in the elevator he would give the guests their key back.

The plan worked very well except for the flood water that would prove to be the operation's undoing. The mysterious floated bottles were taken to Reno Hoag, the hotel owner and manager at the time. He quickly identified the contents, reportedly with some pleasure, considering the stress the high water was causing him on that fateful day. "Skinny's" crime was dealt with quietly relieving him of his duties at the Lafayette. An example to other employees had to be set! Reno of course had to confiscate the bottles in question. "Skinny" was rehired, again quietly, several months later. He eventually graduated from college and went to work for the rapidly expanding Montgomery-Wards Department Store company. "Skinny's" skills in marketing were utilized at Montgomery-Wards where it is said that he worked his way from assistant clerk of the basement paint and hardware department to Executive Vice President of New York Operation in the course of two years.

No mention of "Skinny's" supplier. Could have been one of any number of Beavers—except for "Doc" and Eunice, who never sold from their house. Even at that, they did have some narrow escapes. Happened on one of the few times when they were making their own whiskey "from scratch."

As Eunice told it, "Doc" was in their cellar "running" whiskey ("so the kids wouldn't know"). Eunice was outside hanging out some clothes when two carloads of lawmen stopped in the road below. About two dozen officers got out and proceeded to come up through the yard:

I grabbed some paper boxes and a pair of old rubber overshoes and had a fire going by the time they were coming up through the yard. The smell of those overshoes covered the smell of the whiskey so well that they went right past and up through the woods.

Toward the end, raids like that became more and more frequent. Without warning, groups of lawmen would arrive without notice and "fan out" over the area looking for "moonshiners." When that happened, "everyone gathered up their hoes and rakes and went to work in the corn fields until they left."

Sometimes, officers would go from door to door making inquiries. "See anyone just go by here?" "We'd just say no, and let it go at that."

Along with whiskey, many Beavers also made beer. "Doc" and Eunice excepted. That was about to change. Construction on new Route Seven brought many strangers from Columbus to oversee work. They soon found Beavertown whiskey and consumed their share. However, they missed their beer, available in great quantities at home. One of the bosses approached Eunice and asked if she would make some for them.

"At first, I refused, but they persisted. Finally gave in—making them promise not to tell anyone. I made up a batch and put a little whiskey in it. Made it real good—high test. Made it only for them. I never, never sold locally."

With all the comings and goings some of her beer ended up in Columbus. Not just to Columbus, but all the way into the governor's mansion. Arrangements were soon made for a steady supply. Once a week, in the middle of the night, a big black limousine would drive down from Columbus, drop off cases of empty bottles and pick up full ones.

"Sometimes, the governor himself (Democrat Vic Donahey) came and had a few beers right here at this table."

"Slopy" Cochran happened to pick one of those nights to pay them a visit. Saw the big black car and thought that the law had caught up with them. Almost turned away, but curiosity got the best of him.

Came up the front way and knocked gingerly on the door. Everyone put their bottles under the table while Eunice peeked out to see who it was. Opening the door, she beckoned him in. They all brought out their bottles and asked if he would like one.

"Oh, boy," he said, "those words were music to my ears. I thought sure you'd been caught."

Eunice might have kept on making beer to the bitter end, but one of Beavertown's biggest "blabber mouths" happened in at the wrong time. "I knew that everyone in town would soon know about it, so I poured the whole batch out and quit. And when I quit, I quit."

All through the twenties, whiskey sales kept Beavertown going strong. The crash of 1929 changed all that. Not immediately, but bit by bit, until they were down to "scraping the bottom of the barrel."

On top of that, everyone now had gas and electricity bills to pay. Most of the surrounding farms had free gas. From oil wells drilled on their properties during the big "oil boom" of the late eighteen-hundreds. Several of those wells had been drilled in Beavertown during "Dragon

John's" time. While he lived, those wells kept going. With his death, they had simply "gone to pot."

During the plenty of the twenties, gas companies had also laid pipe lines all through the valley. Electric companies brought power to every house. With plenty of whiskey money coming in, everyone signed up. Now, how to pay these bills with no income at all?

Beavers, adept at dealing with money problems, found a way. Very simply—albeit illegally. At that time, electric meters were simple affairs. Just plain rectangular tin boxes attached to one's house. OFF and ON levers on one side. (Favorite targets for "trick or treaters" on Halloween. They would slip in, pull the lever down and take off. Leaving residents in the dark.)

Easy access to the "works" allowed for "adjustments" to electric bills. With the electric off, all one had to do was keep the measuring disc from turning. Accomplished by simply inserting a tiny piece of wire (called a "jimmy") in its path.

That "jimmy" had to be removed before the next meter reader appeared. One day, removing that "jimmy" completely slipped Eunice's mind. She happened to glance down at the highway. There sat the meter reader's truck.

In a panic, she ran into the kitchen and grabbed the first thing to catch her eye. An old butcher knife. Out onto the porch she flew, yanked the glass covering off the disc, attempted to insert the knife and flip the "jimmy" out. Ensuing shock threw her "clean across the porch." Miraculously, she survived, with no ill effects.

Gas meters were totally sealed affairs, tampering quite impossible. However, neighbors suspected that the meter reader, an ex-"moonshine" customer, might be "cutting Beavers a little slack" in his readings.

Eunice maintained a rigorous schedule all her life. Granddaughter, Eileen Thomas wrote this little sketch about her grandmother's activities:

I remember the evenings with Grandma and Pap, popping pop-corn and listening to the radio, working puzzles, playing cards, stringing green beans, shelling peas, stirring off peach butter and apple butter.

Many people bought Grandma's crocheting; she was known for her large pineapple doilies. She always had a quilt to knot or rug to braid. Her hands were never idle.

She taught me to sew. I made my first dress at the age of nine with her beside me. If you made a mistake, you ripped it out and did it over again.

More than likely, that dress was made out of feed sack material. At that time, most animal feed came in cotton sacks with various designs and colors. A real boon for folks in rural areas, who had many children to clothe, and little money.

In the early forties, when "broomstick" skirts were all the rage, Eunice took pity on one of her young teenage neighbors. Rummaging through her stock of "feed sack" material, she dragged out her old treadle-driven Singer and "whipped up" a skirt for her in no time. Enabling her to go to school "in style" like all the other girls. (Called "broomstick" skirts because, when washed, were to be wound around a broomstick to dry.)

Along with everything else, Eunice still found time to keep a diary (all her life). Weddings, births, deaths, tragic events, even family ailments—she covered them all. Of particular interest, entries written during World War II years. Beginning with January of 1943, this section of that diary: (Exactly as Eunice wrote it.)

1943

January 4 – Mary Howell was here today she was Bill Danver's daughter. We had a nice day.

5 – Gladys Haught's man (Leonard Cole) came home today to see his twin babies.

8 – Dean don't feel so good tonight. Was vaccinated today. Bud wouldn't take it.

9 – Got a letter from Sis Knowlton. Just a reminder of friendship. Margaret and the children came to stay the night. Doodle (Eileen) isn't feeling very good, she was vaccinated too.

13 – Sonny Beaver stopped home today. He is working on a boat, he took Freddy Cline back with him. They sure need good men.

15 – Butchering a pig today. Jiggs and kids are here. Dean and Doodle are sick, they took shots for small pox and typhoid fever.

16 – canned pig today. Annabelle Hutchison and Roy Heiney were married today.

17 – Oscar Mount came home. Was discharged from the army.

18 – Chuck went back on the boat. His time is changed, he gets home every two weeks. Chuck's dad worked on the Duckalite as a deck hand.

February 2 – Bill Mount came home from the army.

5 – War ship went past this morning.

7 – Just received word that Freda Beaver's boy died this morning. He was 14 years old. Shoes were rationed this afternoon—3 pair a year.

13 – Earnest Rosenlieb, Mary Teeman's man came home on furlow today for 14 days.

19 – Alma Beaver was married tonight.

27 – Got word today that Red Stewart's boy is missing in action.

March 11 – Jackalow Beaver was in a bad wreck today.

15 – Esther Newland had a baby girl this morning.

17 – War ship went past.

27 – Mattie Boston, Jim Beaver's sister died today.

April 3 – got word that George Butler is dead, Doc's last uncle on his mother's side.

4 – Cora Beagle died today.

10 – have a new minister, George Mendenhall.

May 25 – Rob Cochran and George Beaver and Walter Beaver left for the army today.

31 – a grayhound bus wreck down by Arthur Holdrens, about everyone was hurt. Fred Heddleston and baby were on it.

June 7 – Went on the hill to Mrs. Hager funeral.

29 – Lyle Beaver went to the army.

July 8 – A boat sank at Lock 16 -The Dawn–this morning.

13 – Herman Haught came home for a furlow of five days.

August 4 – March Cochran died today.

8 – The grayhound bus hit Earnie (Burnie) Beaver and killed him.

10 – Jack Beaver's boy was buried today.

1944

April 1 – Chuck Berga went to the Navy.

May 12 – Chuck came home on furlough, went back May 20. He helped tear our house down while home. Slopy Cochran and Riddle Beaver built it back up in 15 days. We moved into our new home **July** 3 – Ollie Beaver died.

August 20 – Harry Courtney came home today—he was overseas for three years.

September 8 – Doc is eating dinner with Mr. and Mrs. Parr today, their son David is home from the army.

14 – Finished Jiggs cellar today. (Margaret Berga)

1945

January 15 – David Beaver went to service today. Charley (Pratt) Beaver died today. (Shelda Beaver's grandfather.)

12 – Vernon Cochran, Jim Church and Eddie Beaver was called to report to the army on the 21st.

22 – Clarence Thomas left for the army.

1946

August 10 – David Beaver drowned today at Lock 16 in Beavertown. He had been home from the Navy one week.

December 14 – Gene Holdren went into Beaver and Paynter store.

1947

March 8 – Doc and Dean started Johnny's basement for their new home.

April 1 – Big train wreck in Bens Run.

November 22 – Johnny Boy moved into their new home.

1949

October 13 – Doc got his leg broke.

November 4 – Put electric light in church on the hill.

1950

December 11 – Laura Beaver died today.

13 – Danny Beaver went to the army.

1951

March 23 – Bud Beaver went to the army.

August 4 – Bud's 21st birthday, he left for Germany.

1953

February 26 – Paul Beaver went to army.

Like all communities, Beavertown sent many of its young men into battle. After four long years, they came home. Except for Andrew Courtney, who lived about a mile below Beavertown. He died in the D-Day invasion.

GI bonuses helped settle ex-soldiers back into normal life. The G.I. Bill gave many a lift up into better circumstances. Industries geared up for the war now had to "retool," so manufactured goods were in short supply for a spell. New cars had to be ordered, then a long wait. The Hartshorns got tired of waiting for their new Chevy. Broke down and bought one of those new-fangled Kaisers. Which turned out to be something of a "lemon."

In the early fifties, plans were announced for construction of two new aluminum plants up in Hannibal, Ohio. (Within driving distance of Beavertown.) Every able bodied Beaver found good paying jobs there. During construction, and later inside the plant.

Those two plants kept everyone in the valley working and making "good" money for years. Workers even received ten weeks paid vacations periodically. By the time both plants closed in 2000, most Beavers had reached retirement age. Were also receiving Social Security along with pensions. No need for making "moonshine" anymore.

Since he could not pass the eye test, "Doc" Beaver never benefited from those plants, but his children and grandchildren did. Not that he just sat around. He was never without work of some kind. On March 31, 1954, at 8:30 in the morning, he was getting ready to go to work when his heart just stopped. He was only sixty-nine. For the first time in her life, Eunice was alone.

Fortunately, all of her children lived nearby, so she was hardly deserted. She still kept busy. Crocheting those huge pineapple dollies for which she was famous, making braided rugs, etc.

Nor did she confine herself to home. Her interests were many and varied. Not unusual to find her sitting in the grandstand with son, "Bugs," and his daughter, watching the horse races up in Wheeling, West Virginia.

Auctions and garage sales were her passion. Coming from Matamoras one day, she and granddaughter Peggy Taylor stopped at a garage sale. After examining every item carefully, picked up a pair of boy's football shoes.

Peggy was aghast. "Grandma, you're not buying those, are you?"

Eunice drew herself up. "Why," said Eunice, "those would be just the thing to wear when I'm mowing that hilly side of my yard." (She was in her late eighties or early nineties at that time.)

"Put those things back," said Peg. "You'll not be doing any mowing, if I have anything to say about it."

As her eye sight grew worse, she was forced to give up her crocheting. But her mind was clear as a bell, and she loved talking about old times, especially "moonshine" days. Those were the days of the writer's interviews with Eunice. Sometimes she would pause, get a far-away look in her sightless eyes and sigh, "Oh, I guess it wasn't right, but it did put clothes on our kids' backs and shoes on their feet."

She might have continued living there by herself to her very end, had not a couple con-men knocked on her door one day. "Said that they were selling linoleum, and I needed new linoleum, so I let them in."

One kept her busy while the other searched the house. Not until later did she discover that two hundred dollars had been stolen from her purse.

Never felt safe living alone again. Lived with one of her children, then another. Finally, ended up in The Arbors (nursing home) in Marietta, Ohio. By that time, had celebrated her one hundredth birthday. Prominently displayed near her bedside, presidential letter of congratulations for reaching one hundred years of age.

Now totally blind, she had lost none of her mischievous nature. One of her visitors asked, "If you can't see, what in the world do you do all day?" "Oh," said Eunice, with a twinkle in her sightless eyes, "Sometimes I count my fingers."

She died shortly after and was buried up in Parr Hill Cemetery, next to "Doc," just inside the gate. Obituary follows:

OBITUARY

Eunice Beaver, 100, formerly of New Matamoras, died Sunday, Feb. 28 at The Arbors, Marietta.

She was born in Ludlow Township, O., a daughter of the late William and Sarah Hanlon Pritchard.

She was a member of the Beavertown United Methodist Church and a homemaker.

She is survived by two sons, Raymond "Bud" Beaver of Fly, O., Dean Beaver of Newport, a daughter, Mildred Smith, Reno; three sisters, Almeda Pots, Helen Illig and Bertha Beaver, all of East Liverpool, O.; 14 grandchildren; 24 greatgrandchildren; 12 great-great grandchildren and two step great-great grandchildren.

She was preceded in death by her husband, Raymond "Doc" Beaver in 1954; a daughter, Margaret Berga in 1992, a son Vernon "John" Beaver in 1989; six brothers and five sisters.

Funeral services were held Tuesday, March 2 at 2 p.m. at the Ruttencutter Funeral Home with the Rev. Frank Conley officiating. Interment will be in the Parr Hill Cemetery, Beavertown, O. (Courtesy of Barbera Mackey)

CHAPTER 19

*E*unice's death essentially marked the end of old Beavertown, but it had been steadily deteriorating even while she was still there. Her house is now remodeled beyond recognition. William Columbus' house completely gone. A mobile home in its place. Gone, also, "Mutt" Holdren's house. Only "Griz" Beaver's house still stands. Of all those McCall houses, only one remains. Now owned and occupied by Linda Heiney Danver (Great granddaughter of Mima McCall Haught).

Across the little stream, Charlie's Prohibition house still stands. Although he would never recognize it now with its new look. The Jim Wines house, (where "Jiggs" Cochran raised his family) stands empty at this writing. Out of all those Cochran houses, only three remain. Those of Charles Cochran (home to the Bob Bradford family for several years), Ray Cochran (home of Thelma Cochran) and Clarence "Slopy" Cochran (home of Doug and Kathy Cochran).

To the north, mainly empty space. Old McMahan house, once occupied by the John Hutchison family, gone. As is "Riddle's" house, with only a set of broken cement steps remaining—a single bunch of Easter lilies blooms there every Spring.

To the south, empty spaces where four or five houses once stood. John Mounts' grocery store still stands, now home to a family not native to the area. "Billow" Danver's house—also occupied by strangers to the area, but very well kept. Both lock houses—intact, but nowhere near their original state. On the river side, the old lock house (now in private hands) survives in quite good condition. But surrounded by several other smaller dwellings.

Even Beavers themselves, few and far between.

At this writing, of those actually wearing the surname Beaver, and residing in Beavertown, only six:

David Beaver (son of Harry Beaver, son of Fred Beaver, son of William Columbus). Minister of the Parr Hill Community Church.

Lonnie Beaver (son of Veryl "Cotton" Beaver, grandson of William Columbus).

Neil Beaver (son of Cecil "Blackie" Beaver, son of Fred Beaver, son of William Columbus).

Suzanne Beaver (widow of Timothy Beaver, son of Neil Beaver).

Kim Beaver (daughter of Danny Beaver. From another branch of the Beaver family tree).

Thelma Beaver (widow of Bill Beaver, son of Veryl "Cotton" Beaver, grandson of William Columbus).

Beavers not wearing the Beaver surname:

Bob Bradford, (son of Alma Beaver Thomas, daughter of "Junky" Earle Beaver, son of William Columbus).

Todd Bradford and Celesta Bradford Crawford (son and daughter of Bob Bradford)

Dennis and Douglas Berga (sons of James Berga, son of Margaret "Jiggs" Berga, daughter of Raymond "Doc" Beaver, son of William Columbus).

Gary Cochran and Sue Cochran Mahoney (son and daughter of Vernon "Jiggs" Cochran, son of Icy Beaver Cochran, daughter of William Columbus).

Ryan & Brandon Cochran, (sons of Gary Cochran).

Altogether, just fifteen. Almost the same number of Beavers who settled the town way back in 1882.

In spite of all the notoriety, Beavertown's history follows much the same pattern as all others in the county (until Prohibition). A town whose founder and maker was a man called "Dragon John." A unique individual who single handedly built a town out of that scraggly, hilly piece of ground, which thousands of immigrants had passed by without giving it a second look.

Under his guidance and foresight, the town grew and prospered with no help from the outside. Actually, the public at large scarcely noticed it. Maps of the day left it off entirely. (As do most maps today.)

From April 16, 1917, to November 11, 1918, the United States was at war with Germany. Affecting Beavertown little. The period of high living which followed left it out entirely.

Had it not started making "moonshine," there may have been no Beavertown at all. Instead, it not only survived—it would never be forgotten by a grateful clientele.

To demonstrate, a few examples.

Construction Supervisor, "Norm" Hartshorn, worked with men from all parts of the country. No matter where, once workers learned that he lived down along the Ohio River, someone was sure to ask if he "might live anywhere near the little town that made all that whiskey."

That was back in the mid nineteen-hundreds, but even after the turn of the century, no let up.

In the spring of 2009, a couple from Florida purchased a summer home in Matamoras, not far from Beavertown. One of their relatives who lived across the river near St. Marys, West Virginia, said jokingly, "You do know that you're moving up into whiskey country, don't you?" (Matamoras is only six miles north of Beavertown.)

Not long after, a Matamoras family was attending church in Pittsburgh, Pennsylvania. After services, the minister's wife asked them where they lived.

Thinking that Pittsburghers had probably never heard of Matamoras, the mother said, "In a little town down along the Ohio River, about thirty miles north of Marietta."

"Marietta? And where is that?"

The daughter was aghast. *Never heard of the first settlement in the Ohio Territory.* Giggling, she said, "Probably wouldn't know where Beavertown is then."

To their amazement, the lady replied, "Why, yes. Yes, matter of fact, I do.

Sometime later, same family was shopping in Parkersburg, West Virginia. Totaling up their purchases, the elderly clerk asked for name and address.

As she was entering their information, for fun, one daughter quipped, "Guess you never heard of Beavertown either."

Replied the clerk, "I'm not from this area. Just moved here from Charleston. But that name sorta sounds familiar." Little wonder. For thirteen years, the "Cotton" triumvirate sold all of its whiskey to customers from Charleston. "Every week a truck came, pulled up into our garage and loaded up with whiskey." ("Cotton")

December 5, 2018, marked ninety-five years since the repeal of Prohibition. Incidents like those mentioned above have become fewer and fewer. Even *The Marietta Times* seems to have lost interest in "that notorious little moonshine town." Maybe the day will come when no one remembers. Maybe.

The purpose of writing this history is not to remind readers of Beavertown's checkered past, nor to cast aspersions on those long gone. Rather, to throw some light on circumstances which thrust the tiny hamlet into the public eye, and to show what it was like living there in "moonshine" years.

In the 1980's, some of the original "moonshiners" were still living. Neighbors and friends were still full of tales about the way it was back then.

The few Beavers who live there now know little to nothing about the "old times." It has become increasingly harder to find anyone who does. Not impossible.

August, 2019, writer's daughter was conversing with the manager of Wayside Furniture Store in New Martinsville, West Virginia. Talking about the area in general, happened to mention that her mother was writing a book about a little town down river—Beavertown.

"Of course, you're too young to remember anything about Prohibition days," she commented.

"True," the manager agreed. "But my father's sitting right there in the back. We'll ask him."

"Dad, you ever hear of a place called Beavertown?"

"I sure have," said his ninety-year-old father. "I didn't drink much myself, but I used to haul one of my "buddies" down there to buy whiskey. They sure made a lot of it there."

ACKNOWLEDGEMENTS:

Major Contributors

Commentaries by:

Lyle Beaver, who lived his early years in Beavertown, but maintained a close association with them all his life. He was the initial inspiration for this book.

Original "Moonshiners" — Eunice Beaver, Veryl "Cotton" Beaver, Dorthy Beaver.

Interviewed in the 1970's and 1980's, they have long since passed away. It seemed only proper that they should not be forgotten.

Others

Commentaries and contributions by relatives, friends, acquaintances:
Eileen Thomas, genealogist, great, great granddaughter of "Dragon John."
Joanne Cochran
Doug and Cathy Cochran
Paul Beaver
Don Mark Holdren
Pearl Haught

Evelyn Decker
Peggy Taylor
Dianne McMahan
William Beaver
Shelda Cloud
Dean Beaver
Barbera Mackey
Dr. Richard Hamilton
Leo Mack Herrick

Technical Assistance:

Theresa Gautschi and Douglas Hartshorn

BIBLIOGRAPHY

Andrews, Martin R. MA. *History of Marietta and Washington County, Ohio*. Biographical Publishing Company. Chicago, Illinois, 1902.

Atlas of Washington Co. Ohio. Titus, Simmons & Titus. Philadelphia, Pennsylvania. 1875.

Beaver Family History, I.M Beaver, Published 1936.

Behr, Edward. *Prohibition*. Arcade Publishing, New York, 1996.

Brant & Fuller, *History of the Upper Ohio Valley*, Madison, Wis., 1891.

Coffrey, Thomas M. *The Long Thirst*. (Prohibition in America, 1920-1933) W.W. Norton and Company, Inc., New York, 1995.

Galbreath, Charles B. *History of Ohio*. The American Historical Society, Inc. Chicago and New York, 1925.

Grandview Township's First Trustees Journal, 1808-1843. Windmill Publications, Inc., Mt.Vernon, IN.

Havighurst, Walter. *River to the West*, G.P. Putnam & Sons. New York, N.Y. Copyright 1970.

History of the Ordinance of 1787and the Old Northwest Territory. Northwest Territory Celebration Commission, Marietta, Ohio. 1937.

History of Washington County, Ohio. Sponsored by The Washington County Historical Society, Marietta, Ohio. H.Z. Williams & Bro., 1881. Reprint, The Bookmark, Knightstown, Ind.

Howe, Henry, L.L.D. *Historical Collections of Ohio*. State of Ohio, C.J. Krehbiel & Co., Cincinnati, Ohio, 1904.

Kobler. *Ardent Spirits*. G.P. Putnam's Sons, New York, 1973.

Lewis, Thomas William. *History of Southeastern Ohio and the Muskingum Valley*. Volume I. The S.J. Clarke Publishing Co. 1928. Chicago.

Matthews, Alfred. *Ohio and Her Western Reserve*. D. Appleton and Company, New York. 1902.

Muskingum Valley Review, December 10, 2000.

Sinclair, Andrew, *Prohibition*. Atlantic Monthly Press Book. Little, Brown and Company, Boston 1962.

The Marietta Times,700 Channel Lane, Marietta, Ohio.

Van Fosson, William Harvey. *The Story of Ohio*. The Macmillan Company, New York, 1937.

CPSIA information can be obtained
at www.ICGtesting.com
Printed in the USA
BVHW022251131122
651880BV00022B/567

9 781662 853166